RIVER AT THE DOOR

UNUSUAL EXPERIENCES IN ISOLATED AREAS

Allen Anthony

Allen Anthony

River Microstudies
Fort Davis, Texas

Copyright © 1987 by River Microstudies
LC 88--123398
All rights reserved
Printed in the United States of America
Second printing 1989
Third printing 1992
Fourth printing 1997

Cover scene and map, as well as chapter sketches: Susan L. Tanner

ISBN 0--9625865--0--1

ISBN 0--9625865--0--1

ACKNOWLEDGMENTS

Gratitude must be expressed first to all who have provided the material from which the articles in this compilation were prepared. I have drawn widely and fruitfully from the accounts of numerous feature article writers, area staff reporters, and local correspondents for both large and smaller newspapers in the greater region. I am also indebted to many who so generously contributed to this effort through interviews, correspondence, and telephone calls, involving both recollections of bygone days and reports on current circumstances.

I wish to express personal appreciation for the invaluable assistance, in so many and different ways, of such individuals in the study areas as C.M. Walts, Alfred Stepp, Emmett Lewis, Marie Cash, Carolyn Speck, Joanne Moore, Lillian Dawson, Bart Futrell, Ellis B. Tucker, Bill McNichols, Jack Nunn, James H. Williams, Bertha Edmunds, Lena Ezell, Gilbert Moore, and, most recently, Virginia and R.B. Jewell.

Special thanks are also extended to Will Ed Winfield, Cecil Gibbs, and Pat Bagsby for their aid in providing photographs for one article.

I am grateful to the to the various journals, newspapers, and one book publisher, along with their societies and management as appropriate, for permission to reprint previously published articles or to otherwise include content from their publications. In some instances this includes the providing of various photographs and authorization to adapt accompanying maps to provide illustrations within this book. This also includes approval from newspapers to prepare pictures from photocopies made from bound issues or microfilm rolls when original negatives or prints were no longer retained in photo files. This permission made these illustrations possible for inclusion in this volume, despite the loss in quality, when they would otherwise apparently not have been available. Specific credits to these generous parties for their contributions which have made this volume possible are shown at appropriate places within this compilation.

This work would not have been possible without the materials and services provided by efficient staff at many libraries. Assistance given in the facilities at Murray State University was especially helpful.

I am indebted to Dr. Jewell Phelps who guided me during my first venture in research in this field at George Peabody College.

I feel I was most fortunate to have attended Pleasant Grove School, a rural, two-room grade school in Jefferson County, Kentucky, where the influence of Elizabeth W. (Mrs. Robert) Tyler and (Mrs.) Edmonia H. Stout, addressed by their pupils as, respectively, "Miss Whitman" and "Miss Hall", gave capable direction down the beginning path of learning.

I am thankful to my mother, Mrs. Zada H. Anthony, for her nurture and sacrifices during my early years of education.

Finally, I express appreciation to my wife, Elizabeth, my son, Thomas, and my daughter, Susan, for their support and encouragement, including on some occasions their accompaniment and assistance in the field during research.

Contents

Introduction   iii

---

1   Linton Mailboat On The Cumberland: A   3
Link With The Outside World

2   Wolf Island: From A Haven For River   35
Pirates To An Assignment For A
Ferryboat-Commuting Schoolteacher

3   Kentucky Bend: A Little Chip Off The   57
Big Block
     A   Kentucky Bend: A Struggle For   59
        Political Identity
     B   Steamboat 'Round Kentucky Bend -   75
        A Golden Era
     C   Kentucky Bend - The Lock That   87
        Had To Be Released

4   Reverie: A Tennessee Post Office In A   97
Disabled Arkansas School Bus

5   Corona: From The Devil's Elbow Bend To   127
Centennial Island - Almost Overnight

COLUMBUS, KY AS THE NATION'S CAPITAL

Legend or Near Reality?
A Compilation of Accounts

Allen Anthony

ISBN 0-9625865-1-X

Retail $12.95 ● 1994 Distribution ● 1993

RIVER MICROSTUDIES
Box 259
Fort Davis, TX 79734
915/426-3570 (1-5 PM) ● 915/426-3844 FAX

Reviews from Journals:

. . . documents the folklore of the subject as it has been handed down orally and in newspapers for over a century.

. . . this is not your typical local history.

. . . the book is well written and documents the development of a well-worn tale but one little known outside Hickman County.
> — *The Filson Club History Quarterly*

This small book is testimony to the tenacity of a historical legend...

Anthony has compiled all the sources that either propagate or denigrate the legend...

Despite Anthony's throught job...

someone will always believe that a small western Kentucky town almost obtained for itself the designation as our nation's capital.
> — *Register of the Kentucky Historical Society*

RIVER AT THE DOOR

Unusual Experiences
in
Remote Areas
Allen Anthony

ISBN 0-9625865-0-1
Retail $13.95 ● 4th printing ● 1987

RIVER MICROSTUDIES
Box 259
Fort Davis, TX 79734
915/426-3570 (1-5 PM) ● 915/426-3844 FAX

Retailers may special order from
BAKER & TAYLOR
HERVEY'S BOOKLINK
THE SUPREME CO.

Internet/World Wide Web
Viewer Opportunities For Books From
River Microstudies
● Overland Net ● Internet Book Fair
● Book Stacks Unlimited ● BookZone

A Special Book for American History

Reviews from Journals:

. . . an intriguing glimpse . . .
. . . fascinating vignettes . . .
. . . illuminating contexts . . .
—*The Egregious Steamboat Journal*

. . . will delight . . . historians, geologists, sociologists
and folklorists, as well as river enthusiasts . . .
. . . recounts some fascinating stories in an
interesting style . . .
. . . well worth the price .
—*The Register of the Kentucky Historical Society*

INTRODUCTION

Come journey with me in place and time to some "little-known worlds" found in remote if not isolated areas in the valleys of the Cumberland and Mississippi rivers. Largely bypassed by the main avenues of land travel, usually because of the difficulty if not the impossibility of access, these communities generally were dependent upon transportation which could be provided upon the surface of the river - a body which could be both friend and foe as experience of course would prove over the years. Travel by land, where possible, was during early years slow, lengthy and circuitous to reach even county seats, not to mention larger cities elsewhere in the region. The situation in many cases remains the same today.

Located in the narrow-confines of their valleys in generally sparsely settled realms, the inhabitants have displayed evidence of individuality, fierce determination, and local as well as state pride and loyalty. The physical environments often differed among these various communities. Residents in some instances had chosen to settle on an already-existing island. In some cases settlers living within a meander of the river eventually, and on one occasion suddenly, found themselves occupants of a newly-formed island. Often the residents were left on the "wrong" side of the river, attached to or at least more closely linked with a neighboring state instead of their former homeland. Sometimes state boundary line determinations and even Supreme Court decisions have been involved in the eventual status of these displaced citizens.

I have not reached out in writing to some other areas that would qualify for inclusion. Considerable attention has been given by numerous other investigators to the rather well-known Kaskaskia Island of Illinois, with its historic settlements of Kaskaskia and Pujol. Over the years writers for the Memphis papers have reported upon Tennessee's Island No. 40, which once had a Bull Pen Landing, on the Arkansas side of the river immediately upstream from that large city. The perhaps less-familiar Davis Bend of Mississippi, once containing the small settlement of Palmyra and now severed to be on the Louisiana side, suggests another possibility - perhaps among others.

While it might be contended that there is only a limited impression of a sense of cohesion or even unity apparent with in this assemblage of studies done upon somewhat scattered communities located in two separate river valleys, it is nevertheless true that these localities have shared a number of common experiences emanating from the effects of riverine environments. At any rate, these various accounts will be permitted to tell their own stories in turn.

Let us now prepare to drift downstream on the Cumberland River from Nashville, by Clarksville, to the three communities of Dover and Tobaccoport in Tennessee and, just over the state line, Linton in Kentucky, where small, homemade mailboats once provided vital services to those along this stream. A somewhat lengthy trip thereafter downriver to the junction with the Ohio River and then westward to the confluence with the Mississippi River will next bring us a few miles down this major stream to Wolf Island, which became caught in the grasp of a struggle for political and economic possession between Kentucky and Missouri. Our next landing will be at the unique site of Kentucky Bend, a loop of the Mississippi belonging to Kentucky, but surrounded by Missouri and Tennessee and completely isolated from the remainder of its state. We will afterwards wind our way downstream to the community of Reverie on Island No. 37, once connected directly by land across its meander in the river to its county seat in Tennessee but now closely linked with a nearby town on the mainland of Arkansas. Our final port of call will be Corona, presently situated on Centennial Island after a flooding Mississippi cut across a narrow neck of land and eventually cast this settlement, still a part of Tennessee, toward the Arkansas shoreline. You may wish to disembark later in Memphis.

Ready? The idling engine of the old steamboat has had the paddlewheel turning slowly. If all are aboard, let's blow the ship's whistle , sound the bell, unfasten the line from the mooring, pull away from the landing, raise the gangplank into position - and be on our way!

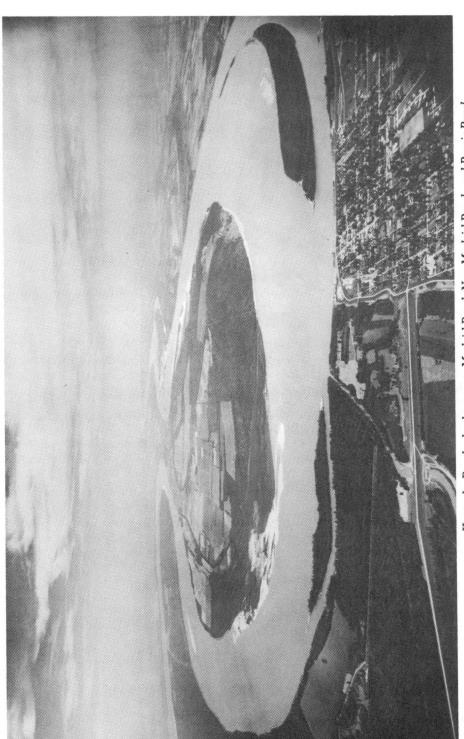

Kentucky Bend, also known as Madrid Bend, New Madrid Bend, and Bessie Bend

"The Linton Mailboat on the Cumberland River: A Link With The Outside World", by Allen Anthony is reprinted from *The Filson Club History Quarterly,* ©1985, Volume 59, No. 1 (January 1985), pp. 5-39, by permission of The Filson Club.

1

DOVER AND TOBACCOPORT, TENNESSEE; LINTON, KENTUCKY

The Linton Mailboat On The Cumberland River: A Link With The Outside World

The year 1889 was remembered by river men as the final big year before a decline in traffic commenced on the lower Cumberland River (Fig. 1) between Nashville, Tennessee, and Smithland, Kentucky, the point of junction with the Ohio River.[1] By 1913 only the Cumberland River Steamboat Company and the new Ryman Line survived as regular operators on this portion of the river.[2] Seven years later steamboats along this stretch "were getting to be as scarce as the proverbial hen's teeth."[3] Between 1920 and 1930 only a few steamboats still operated on the lower Cumberland. A limited number of gasoline-powered tow-boats had made their appearance during this time, but even these vessels soon began to disappear as a result of declining business along the river.[4]

It was during this latter era, however, that mail transportation by power boats on the nation's inland waterways represented a significant and vital operation as a service of the United Stated Post Office Department. For instance at the end of the fiscal year 1924 power boats were operating over 285 routes extending over 55,797 miles representing an expenditure of $1,440,322.[5]

One such route was established along the lower Cumberland River to connect Linton, Kentucky, with Dover, Tennessee (Fig. 2). These two small towns, located at the river's edge in their respective counties of Trigg and Stewart which share the common border of their states, were about twenty miles apart. The only other community located along the river between Linton and Dover that might have qualified as a small town was Tobaccoport, Tennessee, about four miles south of Linton on the same side of the Cumberland.

Linton, first known as Olive's Landing and later as Shipsport, had served as a steamboat landing as early as 1820.[6] During the early decades of the twentieth century, Linton was remembered as a bustling community served by two hotels, five stores, two blacksmith shops, a livery stable, and an iron furnace - as well as being home for between seventy-five and one hundred people.[7] Another early resident of the area recalled that Linton, "almost as big as Dover" at that time, also had a barber shop, while Tobaccoport supported three grocery stores.[8] Still another valley resident and river traveler during this era remem-

Fig. 1 - Lower Cumberland Valley
Adapted from County Map of Kentucky and Tennessee in *Mitchells's New General Atlas* (Philadelphia, 1865), p. 28.

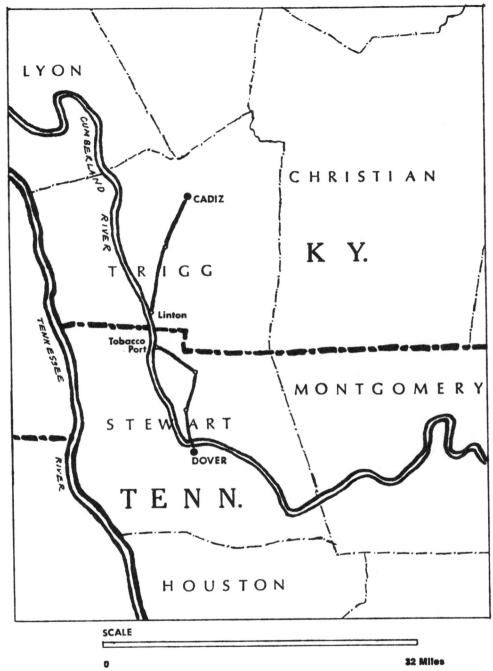

Fig. 2 - The area in 1878
Adapted from Post Route Map of the States of Kentucky and Tennessee with Parts of
Adjacent States by W. L. Nicholson, Topographer of Post Office Department, designed
and constructed under the orders of Postmaster General David M. Key.

5

bered that in the closing years of steamboat service perhaps only one vessel a week, such as the *Idlewild* which operated on the Cumberland at that time, stopped at landings to load such cargo as cattle and grain.[9] Other recollections and illustrations from this period suggest a continued shipping of railroad ties prepared from the timber cut in this region.

ROUTES, LANDINGS, AND SCHEDULES

It was in this setting that the need for improved postal service, as well as for more convenient travel, was recognized during the second decade of the century. Until at least 1912 the only mail service for Linton was provided by an "overland" star route extending to the northeast through the small communities of Donaldson and Maple Grove to Cadiz, the county seat (Fig.3).[10] The carrying of the mail was provided at first by horseback riders and later by horse and buggy conveyance.[11] If this route was continued during the years that followed, its service was neither as frequent nor as satisfactory as that which was afforded by the new river route that was soon established.[12] The mailboat operation was initiated to increase the service for the area to six days a week and to provide better connections through interchange with postal routes southward in Tennessee.[13] When this new route was established, it extended from Linton upriver to Dover, where it connected with another route which ran further upstream to Cumberland City.[14] This Stewart County town was located on the Louisville and Nashville Railroad's Bowling Green-Memphis line offering direct daily mail connections with places across the nation.[15]

The connecting Dover-Cumberland City route was served by larger mailboats which carried both mail and passengers. One such vessel was *The Dispatch*, which reportedly operated seven days a week.[16] Another was the *Estelle Davis*. Mailboats continued to serve on this portion of the Cumberland until at least 1928.[17] One such craft was remembered as having a pilot house.[18] This or a similar boat during this period was estimated to have accommodated as many as fifty passengers.[19]

The beginning date of the operation of mailboat service between Linton and Dover remains unknown or at least uncertain. Official records covering power boat routes of the Post Office Department cover only the period 1920-1944, but this does not eliminate the possibility that such service may have occurred earlier.[20] In fact several residents of the area during this period believed that the Linton mailboat began operation as early as 1910, 1912, 1914, 1915, or at least "during the teens."[21] The Post Office Department records confirm that at least by 1920 the Linton mailboat was operating to serve Route No. 27098 from "Linton (KY.), by Tobaccoport, to Dover, Tennessee, and back, six times a week. . . ."[22]

Regardless of the exact year, the initiation of service by the Linton mailboat was to usher in a new era for the inhabitants of this part of the lower Cumberland Valley that had no earlier - or later - counterpart. Steamboats in the previous decades had not really provided such local service to small landings nor

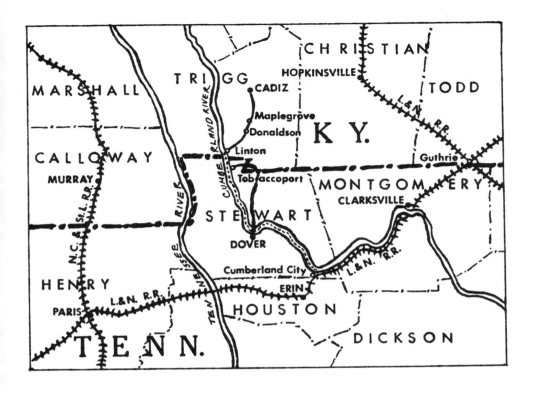

Fig. 3 - Postal service for the area in 1915
Adapted from Post Route Map of the States of Kentucky and Tennessee with the Intermediate Distances on Mail Routes in Operation on the 1st of April, 1915, published by order of Postmaster General A. S. Burleson.

had they been able to render such a personal touch to the lives of the residents. In later years the increased use of automobiles, including those used by mail carriers, to provide links with the inland towns failed to maintain that special sense of participation known in this period.

The mailboat served small post offices, typically located in a store near the landings, not only in the route's terminal towns of Linton and Dover but also in Tobaccoport. In addition, the mailboat carried passengers between these three communities and stopped on signal to board and discharge riders at numerous landings lying along the route. These informal "ports of call," usually serving the farm families on whose property they were established or connecting with rural, unimproved roads ending at the river's edge, were located on both banks of the Cumberland (Fig. 4). Among such landings shown on the few surviving maps and recalled by residents of this period were: Lineport, Cherry's Riverside, Acree's, Neville's, Walker's, Elliott's, Nolan's, Sykes', Brandon's, Moore's, Old Jackson's (later Fitzhugh's), Brewer's, Kelley's, Stall's, Stile's, Pace's,

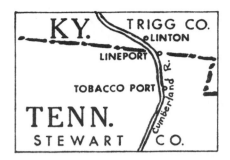

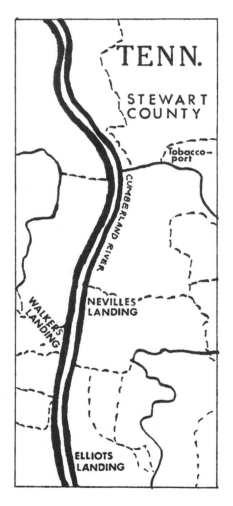

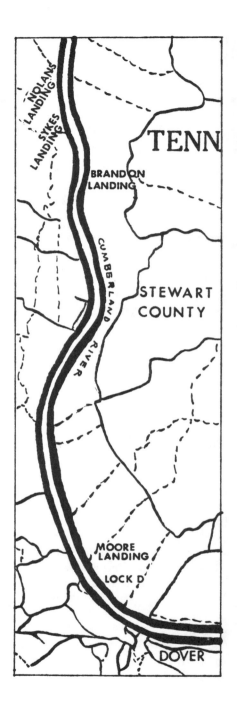

Fig. 4 - Landings along the Cumberland served by the Mailboat
Adapted from Map of Kentucky by W. C. Eyl, Lexington, Kentucky, 1922 and Map of
Stewart County by Walter F. Pond, Nashville, Tennessee, 1937.

Spiceland, and Lower Dover.[23] Some of the landings may have been known by more than one name due to changes in land ownership during the period.

Landings used by the mailboats were usually very simple facilities, being little more than convenient bank sites where the craft could find easy access. These small boats were tied by rope to a stob or a tree near the river's edge where a plank was often used as a "gangplank" to make it easier for older passengers to "bridge the gap." Younger riders usually jumped the intervening distance, at least when leaving the vessel.[24]

At the larger towns where steamboats still called during the earlier years of this era and where barges and similar vessels were tied for loading of goods for shipment (such as ties), facilities and operations were more complex. At Linton the mailboats tied in below the ferry landing where a small craft provided service to the opposite bank to a connecting road.[25] At Dover the mailboats also landed just below a ferryboat landing at the Lower Landing.[26] The larger mailboats operating between Dover and Cumberland City reportedly used the Upper Landing at Dover, so passengers needing connecting service apparently walked the intervening distance between the two landing sites.[27] One rider believed, however, that the two mailboats tied in side by side at the same landing at Dover when he was a patron.[28]

Operations of the boats up and down the river were affected in part by local conditions as well as the whims of the boat operators. When the current was swift the mailboats held closer to shore than did steamboats passing at the same time.[29] When the steamboats and mailboats were in the same area, the much smaller mailboats pulled as far away as possible from the steamboats in order to avoid the backwash waves in the narrow river.[30] Since darkness was encountered at the beginning and end of runs during the winter months, one would think that running lights were mounted on the craft. However, one boat operator reported that he "felt his way" with the aid of whatever reflecting, glimmering light was discernible from the middle of the river! A lantern was carried on top of the cabin but only as a warning or identifying signal for other vessels.[31]

Perhaps the most eventful as well as time-consuming procedure was passage through Lock D, located along the southwestern shoreline of the Cumberland about a mile below Dover (Fig. 4). This facility, completed in 1916, permitted raising or lowering of vessels around the dam which provided flood control and channel depth regulation for this section of the river. Such required passage represented the loss of an hour or longer in "locking through," according to one passenger, and was "an inconvenience" - even if a necessary one.[32] The time lost may have varied depending upon traffic conditions and the speed of the lock operators, since another rider recalled the total passing-through time as averaging only about twenty minutes.[33] One of the boat operators recalled that during the early year of this era, when Cecil Gibbs, assisted by Gibbs Stone, was the lockmaster, mailboats paid no lock fee since their operators helped open up the gates to lock through "the pit."[34]

T. G. WINFIELD'S MAILBOAT
ON THE CUMBERLAND RIVER
AT LINTON IN 1920
Courtesy of Will Ed Winfield

The daily schedule established by the Post Office Department for the conveyance of mail on Route 27098 was shown for a typical year as follows:

Leave Linton (Ky.) daily, except Sunday, 7 a.m.;
Arrive at Dover by 11:30 a.m.;
Leave Dover daily, except Sunday, upon receipt of mail from Cumberland City, but not later than 2:30 p.m.;
Arrive at Linton in 3 hours.[35]

The full 1924 postal service for Linton was shown by the Post Office Department in the following schedule:

Gracey

Via Gracey & Cadiz C.P.
Cadiz 7:30 a.m.

Linton . . . .

Bowling Green & Memphis
Clarksville to Paris
Cumberland City
Tenn., 9:15 a.m.[36]

10

Lantern on the mailboat's cabin as warning to other craft

The routing shown through Gracey apparently represented the earlier, more limited service maintained during this era which extended from Cadiz to the small town of Gracey lying to the east at the junction of the Cadiz Railroad, the Illinois Central Railroad, and the Louisville and Nashville Railroad. This link provided connections to nearby Hopkinsville and points beyond as well as probably providing connections northward to Evansville, Indiana, and southward to Nashville, Tennessee. The second entry in the schedule represented the more valuable mailboat route from Linton to Dover with the connection to Cumberland City on the Louisville and Nashville Railroad's Clarksville-Paris section of the line's Bowling Green - Memphis division.

The mailboats travelled about four miles an hour depending upon direction and river conditions.[37] For instance, the arrival time in Dover, according to one boat operator, depended upon "whether the current was swift."[38] On a day-to-day basis schedules were remembered as being very irregular on this route. One frequent rider recalled, "You never knew when they [the mailboats] would come.

Lock D below Dover

Courtesy of Cecil Gibbs and Pat Bagsby

I don't know that they ever failed to make it, but it was mighty late sometimes."[39] This recollection suggests a different impression of the operation of these smaller Cumberland River mailboats than that provided by Helen Crocker's description of the apparently high-powered "fast little mailboats" on the Green River where "contemporaries recalled that the mailboats were so prompt that river people set their watches by them."[40]

Sometimes the schedules were modified to serve the convenience of the passengers or the whims of the boat operators. For example, the return trip from Dover, according to one resident, was delayed on one occasion while the vessel waited for a rider to return from a dental appointment.[41] This same resident, whose father had been the postmaster at Linton, claimed that his parents sometimes had to wait up until 11:00 P.M. for mail if the boat operator had "taken a notion" to fish enroute or to raid a watermelon patch along the shoreline.[42] Mechanical failures, though not frequent, could also delay the mailboats. One operator recalled, "I've been 12 o'clock at night getting in after having a breakdown."[43]

OPERATORS OR DRIVERS

Although one contemporary believed that the operators of these mailboats were referred to as pilots, others more frequently called them drivers - since in fact they did "drive" these small crafts up and down the Cumberland in much the manner as one would have maneuvered an early automobile within the bounds of a wide dirt or gravel road.[44] (A half steering wheel, simple gear selections, and horsepower similarity help support the analogy.)

One resident thought of the drivers as "river rats" who gained their description from the duties of operating and servicing their often greasy craft. In this characterization he insisted that these operators "were not pilots, but were just river rats, greasy from head to foot. They had to be to keep that old motor running. They had to be a mechanic, had to know the river, had to put in a long day and a long night."[45] Other passengers and the drivers themselves did not recall quite so messy an appearance, but it was clear that the drivers were obligated to assume duties which did not always leave them neat and tidy. At any rate, one passenger recalled the operators as being very congenial and having good personalities.[46]

While drivers who secured the contracts from the Post Office Department had these annual payments as their primary income, they supplemented it from the fares they charged their passengers. Although the amounts varied over the years according to distance, drivers and riders mentioned charges ranging from a quarter to two dollars. Temporary or substitute drivers, sometimes referred to as hired hands since they did not own the boats, did not keep the fares but turned them over to the owners and were compensated with a daily wage of one dollar - at least in the experience of one such hired driver who recalled collecting up to ten dollars a day.[47]

Low-bid awards for mail service contracts on Route 27098 during the period covered by Post Office Department records show the following annual figures.[48]

Contract Years	Awardee	Annual Payment
1920-24	Houston Winfield	$694.50
1924-28	C. C. Hogan	$650.00
1928-32	Millard Cherry	$612.25
1932-36	Millard Cherry	$612.25

In addition to the contract holders shown above (who themselves sometimes drove their boats), there were a number of other drivers who served as temporary or substitute operators. It is likely that Grady (Doc) Winfield drove most of the runs for his father, Houston Winfield, whenever hired operators were not used during the first contract period. It seems likely that one or two persons had operated mailboats under contract during the decade before 1920 when the Post Office Department records begin. If this is so, two early drivers would have been Ed Bogard and C. C. Hogan, the latter during a contract term prior to the one in the record period shown 1924-28.[49] If these men did not actually drive their own boats, they operated boats for others. Other drivers mentioned for this period include: Milburn Lawrence, Newton Lewis, Joe Ahart, Bill Burn Futrell, Chandler Dycus, Burt Sumner, James Halley "Jellybean" Williams, Calvin Doowester, John Moore, Gilbert Moore, and Jack Cherry.[50]

T. G. Winfield, mailboat operator, at Linton about 1920.

Courtesy of Will Ed Winfield

DESCRIPTIONS OF BOATS

The craft used in operation on Route 27098 were small, homemade, and simply designed, varying as a result of the skill and the inclinations of the builders. Each vessel in use at a given time was referred to as the Linton mailboat, or simply as "the mailboat."[51] While only one boat had this distinction, there was often a substitute boat that could be pressed into service when necessary.[52]

The mailboats were constructed in at least two different kinds of buildings. At least one vessel was built in Houston Winfield's blacksmith shop in Linton.[53] Several other boats were made by the Cherry brothers in their tobacco barn located across the river from Linton some distance from the shore. These craft were then moved on tobacco wagons to the river's edge for launching.[54]

Though some of the boats may have been built "from scratch," one builder remembered that basic plans or blueprints were ordered as guidelines. The craftsmen then cut the log, had it sawed and planed, and then field-dried the material themselves. Subsequent steps in construction included cutting the headblock, "notching in on it" for the plank connections, and fashioning the covering bow.[55] One early passenger recalled a "model bow" (V-type) which parted the water with a square or straight-across deck above at the front of the vessel to provide space for passengers entering or leaving the boat.[56]

Boat colors varied among the craft and over the years. One early resident of Linton recalled an impression of gray or blue with the cabin portion having been highlighted in white.[57] When repainting became advisable after a few years of operation, one procedure for "dry-docking" involved winching the vessel out of the water upon two sets of wheels and pulling it up the slope on a track, possibly made of steel.[58]

The length of the boats varied from eighteen to twenty-four feet (with twenty feet as the most common estimate); the width was about eight feet.[59]

Inside the hull two steps descended to the interior of the cabin through a set of doors, opening outward.[60] The newer mailboats usually had windows in the upper parts of these doors to improve visibility when the doors were closed during operation. The roof section at the front of the cabin was raised so passengers would not bump their heads. Another pair of doors was located at the back of the cabin. Both pairs of doors could be opened in the summer.[61] A different recollection was that the back doors were not opened and were provided only for emergency use.[62] Sliding windows in later models were built along the sides of the cabin, replacing the fixed windows of earlier vessels.[63]

Benches for passengers were built along the sides of the cabins and apparently in some models also across the back of the interior under or at the base of the rear doors. Descriptions ranged from "stripped, varnished wood benches" providing a "neat and attractive" accommodation to "slat-type benches like church seats, which were painted red."[64] At least in later years life jackets, provided for safety, were used as padding on the benches - to the relief of weary riders.[65] Recollections of passenger capacity varied from as few as six to eight through twelve to fifteen up to as many as twenty-five around the benches plus

Houston Winfield's blacksmith shop at Linton, Kentucky where T. G. Winfield's mailboat was built about 1918

Courtesy of Will Ed Winfield

additional riders on stools as well as others outside on the back edge of the boat with their "feet hanging out in the water."[66]

Near the center of the cabin, according to most recollections, was a small stove for use during the colder months. One resident contended there was no stove aboard even for use in the winter.[67] Another, however, vividly recalled not only the stove but the fuels used, though memories varied considerably on this point. Wood and coal were burned, though one person suggested that coal oil might have been used at one time instead of wood.[68] Others stressed the importance of wood since coal was not generally available in the area until the late 1930's, remembered that wood was the fuel except when coal was available - and affordable - suggested that both wood and coal were burned, or argued that coal was essential since "wood wouldn't have lasted long enough to put it in," while the boats could carry enough coal to last about a week.[69]

Near the middle of the cabin just forward of the stove was the exposed portion of the engine. A guard was in place over the flywheel to protect the latter from misdirected feet. An exhaust pipe extended from the engine to one side of the vessel with a box structure over it to protect against its heat. The engine hous-

T. G. Winfield in the doorway of his mailboat at Linton in 1920

Courtesy of Will Ed Winfield

ing extended downward into a double hull, which resulted in a "false bottom" feature.[70] Since water gradually seeped into this hidden section, a pump had to be used to remove it from around the flywheel. Normally this procedure was required only before departure each morning and did not have to be repeated enroute.[71] At least some of the boats had a device called a "log-jumper" attached along the length of the bottom to protect the propeller, located toward the rear of the bottom of the hull, against obstructions.[72]

The steering mechanism apparently changed over the years. Descriptions included a simple "rudder cable for steering," the use of a "half-wheel," a "full wheel on the side of the boat by which a roller operated a cord that went back to the rudder," and the later use of a wheel from an old T-model to wind the rope for steering."[73] A gear lever provided for shifting through positions of reverse, forward low, and forward second.[74] One rider remembered the driver sitting with his head out the window when the weather was warm and using the rope extending along the inside of the cabin to the propeller tiller to steer. In cold weather, however, he stood up behind the wheel to steer.[75] Power was provided by gasoline engines, either Clark or Mink two-cylinder, four-horsepower engines, although one driver did mention a five-horsepower Mink engine.[76]

17

Another operator recalled that he liked the Clark engine better even though a boat driven by that engine tended to "hit shore" harder than one powered by a Mink engine.[77] This driver's brother, Millard Cherry, who was also an operator, was remembered by a third driver as having made a boat equipped with a more powerful engine taken from an automobile. It used too much fuel and proved too expensive, however, so Cherry went back to his original vessel powered by the smaller Clark engine.[78]

The little mailboats were not only a familiar sight to residents along the river, but they were also a familiar sound. A Tobaccoport native recalled being able to hear the "put-put-put" of the two-cylinder engine while the boat was still a mile away from where he was fishing along the bank.[79] A lady living near Riverside Landing remembered that she did not have to go outside her house to hear that familiar rhythm as the mailboats passed up and down the river.[80]

One of the drivers believed that the mailboats might have been required to have registration numbers assigned to them, but he did not recall any such numbers lettered on the boats themselves.[81] A passenger remembered that numbers were required as markings in later years of operation at the same time that red/green running lights had to be mounted on the front of the mailboats to meet safety regulations.[82] An operator during the closing years of service believed these craft might have been equipped with a small bell - but he was not certain on this point.[83] Others did not recall markings or lights.

The mailboats themselves certainly left their impressions in the memories of those who were affected by their operation. Most recollections were positive in retrospect. The majority of patrons, as well as drivers, believed that the service was satisfactory, that the boats were rather smooth in their operation for the times, and that the communities were appreciative of the benefits. Favorable comments reflected memories that the boats were comfortable, that their interiors were clean, and that they seldom broke down.[84] A less endearing but perhaps more realistic observation by one who was close to the scene characterized the boats as "full of water, common, homemade, top-heavy, always nasty, slow, noisy, and late." This contemporary also recalled that there were problems at times with the weight distribution of the passengers. In rather picturesque fashion he claimed that "the boat rocked if the driver shifted his tobacco from one cheek to the other."[85]

CONDITIONS AND FACILITIES ABOARD

Obviously space was rather limited in the cabins of these small boats. Apart from mail and other possible cargo as well as the engine and the stove, the area for the passengers was restricted largely to the opposing or encircling benches around the sides of the cabin. Some riders might have sat on stools in the middle of the cabin and even across the back of the end of the boat outside, but this was unusual. Though it does not seem probable that passengers regularly stood when the boat was crowded, one person recalled that the riders "sat down if they could find a place to sit down without sitting in the grease."[86]

If passengers in good weather were able to ride outside the cabin, they could have sat down only if they had used newspapers to cover the grease that was also present there.[87] One rider remembered that children were not allowed to sit across the back of the vessel and dangle their feet in the water.[88] In contrast, another person contended that the boat's propeller was located far enough under water that it would have been safe for children to have dangled their feet overboard. Regardless of the safety issue, it appears this was not usually done - at least when the boat was moving.[89]

Clearly the mailboats were not miniature steamboats in terms of dining and restroom facilities. Normally meals were not consumed on board since the boats' schedules of operation fell between them. If snacks were eaten, they were brought along in a box or pail by the travelers. One driver reported that during his term of service no drinking water was provided for the passenger during runs of up to four or five hours.[90] Another operator believed that riders might have brought their own water jugs.[91] One person recalled that a common water bucket and dipper were kept aboard and re-supplied at Brandon Springs, near Tobaccoport.[92] Two contemporaries recalled the possibility that some passengers drank directly from the river.[93]

A problem surely existed in regard to the unavailability of restroom facilities - not to mention at the landings as well. If a passenger needed to "answer nature's call," he simply had to wait until he got to his destination.[94] A driver believed that passengers in this plight could either wait or secure relief from the back of the boat.[95] Another person suggested that this solution was acceptable only when all passengers were males. In mixed company, however, one asked the operator to make an unscheduled landing or at least to stop longer at a regular landing for relief behind the bushes somewhere near the bank.[96] Another contemporary, however, recalled that mailboats did not stay long enough at scheduled landings to allow for such activities.[97]

REASONS FOR TRAVEL

Passengers were taken on and let off not only at the three post office towns and the often rustic landings in between, but they were also accommodated at any accessible site along the shoreline - anywhere they waved from the bank or told the driver where they wanted off.[98]

All kinds of people rode the mailboats. Most were middle-aged. Both "white and colored" were accommodated during this period.[99] Though men may have been more numerous, women were certainly well represented. Children at times rode in significant numbers. Anybody that wanted to could ride.[100] People rode the mailboat for many reasons. Linton residents took the boat to Dover to visit their dentist, Dr. Henry Crow, who had an excellent reputation in the region.[101] Others went to Dover to see a doctor. On such occasions these patients tried to secure treatment during the boat's midday stay, but if this proved impossible they spent the night and caught the mailboat back the next day.[102] Many passengers were Tennesseans going to and from Dover not only to shop but also to transact legal business involving deeds and taxes since this town was their county seat.[103] Kentuckians from the Linton area often went to Dover to get married, or at least secure the marriage license, not only because of the convenience of travel but also because the waiting period was shorter in Tennessee.[104]

Others rode to and from work and to visit relatives, sometimes crossing the state line in doing so. A minister who lived at Indian Mound across the river north of Cumberland City at one time either used the combination of the two connecting mailboats from that river town or went westward directly to Dover to travel on Saturday to the Linton area to preach in a local church on Sunday. Then on Monday he reversed his route to return to his home in Tennessee.[105] During this period racial prejudice was still strong in some communities of the area. On one occasion workers on a farm near the river toiled until a later hour than was customary. A black laborer who would ordinarily have ridden on a tobacco wagon with a number of whites through the community of Podnick was afraid to pass through that settlement in the company of white passengers on the wagon after dark. Before the wagon departed, he borrowed money from one of the white men to ride the mailboat to his nearest landing since he felt safe on that route.[106] One former Linton resident recalled traveling on "that old boat" many times to a landing between Tobaccoport and Dover near which her parents lived. She took along her three small children, and after leaving the mailboat they walked inland the rest of the way to her childhood home where they visited.[107]

During at least the early part of this era, when automobiles were few in number and rural roads to larger towns were not very dependable where they even existed, the Linton mailboat was the primary, if not the only, conveyance for residents in traveling any significant distance. The railroad link at Cumberland City provided direct connections with no more than a one day layover. One boat rider recalled taking the circuitous route from Tobaccoport to and from Murray, Kentucky, where he attended college. The distance "as the crow flies" was about forty miles. In leaving his home he rode to Dover and changed boats to go on to Cumberland City. There he caught a Louisville and Nashville train to Paris, Tennessee (Fig. 3), where he changed to a Nashville, Chattanooga, and St. Louis train for the remainder of the trip back north to Murray. His brother also rode the mailboats to and from Cumberland City for the train connections to his job in Detroit when he came home for visits.[108] Residents in the Linton area who went to college in Bowling Green also used the mailboat-train connection through Cumberland City.[109] Sometimes the mailboat served as a platform for swimming for young people when the boat was tied at a landing. This opportunity was probably greatest at the Linton landing over the weekends during the summer.[110]

Since the mailboat was not scheduled for mail route trips to Dover on Sunday, it was at times chartered by Linton residents to take groups to church services in Tobaccoport.[111] On special occasions in the summer community groups hired the driver to take them on upriver outings to the Three Sisters Spring. Tubs for great quantities of lemonade were put aboard as part of the provision for a grand picnic. From the spring site the young people wandered off in pairs for "sparking." It was a big day for all.[112]

PERSONAL RECOLLECTIONS

Both passengers and drivers of the mailboats later recalled specific experiences involving them. Some events were pleasant, even humorous; others were sad and sometimes frightening. Gray Acree remembered that when he rode on the boat a sleepy driver often permitted him to operate the craft while he napped on the mail bags. In return, Acree then had his fare waived. Acree recalled a trip on December 22 in either 1916 or 1917:

> . . . we were late due to motor trouble and about dark on our way to Linton we were caught in a severe storm and tied up about one-half way on our trip . . . at Pace's Landing.
> Heat was playing out (an oil heater) but clearing up some after 2 hours tied up . . . so we headed down stream. The storm confused [the driver] so he didn't know up river from down so I directed him and he was acquainted with where we were when I left him.[113]

Clarence L. Cherry, a part time driver, mentioned a rather alarming incident at Ross Bend when a large government towboat caused such an onslaught of high waves that he quickly had to close the boat's front doors because the water was sweeping across the bow.[114]

George Moore, a substitute operator, told of the time a spark plug failed. The driver repeatedly cleaned and reset the spark plug in an attempt to keep the engine running. Eventually it broke. The driver broke off a small branch from an overhanging willow tree and quickly carved a wooden plug. Though this wooden plug provided no firepower, it did prevent further loss of compression and permitted the boat to resume its trip though with reduced engine efficiency. Ultimately the heat caused the wooden plug to ignite. Finally a steamboat, a less common sight in those years, came along and gave him a real spark plug which permitted the run to continue.[115]

Bertha Edmunds, a frequent passenger, recalled when an engine "had played out." When the boat did not arrive at its scheduled landing others went out in another boat to search for it. It was later found adrift downstream and towed back to the landing.[116]

James H. "Jellybean" Williams, a driver, was operating the mailboat on its return from Dover when a fish net became entangled in the screw wheel just upstream from the site of Lock D. The craft became disabled and almost went over the dam extending across the river from the lock. After he managed to secure the boat, Williams arranged through the lockmaster to get word to Dover requesting a flatbed truck. The mailboat was brought to shore and loaded on the truck for the return trip to Dover for repairs.[117] Williams also remembered another occasion when a mailboat partially sank - fortunately within jumping distance of the landing. The passengers and the mail bags were quickly removed, and the half-submerged vessel was pulled ashore.[118]

Jack Nunn recalled the time when a girl who lived in Tobaccoport was suffering from appendicitis. Apparently the nearest, or at least the preferred, hospital was in Hopkinsville. The girl was put on the mailboat to Linton; from there she was taken as quickly as possible to Hopkinsville by way of Cadiz. She almost died. The incident was memorable to Nunn for he later married the girl.[119]

Lena Ezell recalled an emergency which had a sad ending. Her little brother became very ill with diphtheria, then commonly called "membrane croup." The family had the mailboat driver pick up some medicine in Dover. The operator delivered the medicine that evening, but the boy died. The family felt the medicine was "too old" to be effective.[120]

Bill McNichols lived in Linton and his girlfriend lived in Tobaccoport. Both eagerly awaited the arrival of the boat bearing their letters. The couple eventually married as the result of courtship via the mailboat.[121]

Lena Ezell recalled another event with a happier ending. As the former Lena Moore, she lived at Riverside from 1914 to 1916. On the memorable day of May 30, 1915, she and her fiancee, Charlie Ezell, departed on Ed Bogard's mailboat for Dover where the couple was married in the hotel by the river. The bride's sister and the boat driver's wife accompanied the wedding party. Afterwards they caught the boat's return run to Riverside and honeymooned with overnight visits at the homes of their parents.[122]

Will E. Winfield reported that his aunt, then Ruby Stall, was married in a ceremony aboard Ed Bogard's mailboat docked at the Linton landing in 1920. The vessel thus served as the "wedding chapel" with a Reverend Dycus of the local Methodist church officiating. Also aboard for the occasion, in addition to groom Peck Stevens, were the bride's sister, Ludie, and her future husband, T. G. Winfield (the next mailboat driver) as well as the groom's brother and another couple.[123]

George Moore, whose difficulties with a defective spark plug were described earlier, was involved in another incident related to the mailboat operation. He was returning by train from a distant visit and was supposed to get off in Hopkinsville and then make his way to his home in Linton. However, he overslept his getting-off stop and was not awakened by the conductor until the train was almost to Guthrie, Kentucky (Fig. 3). The conductor gave him a pass to catch another train from Guthrie to Erin, Tennessee, where he boarded a hack ("a little motor bus") which took him back north to Dover. There he got on the mailboat to return to Linton - at last.[124]

MAILBOAT CARGOS

Though passengers represented an important part of the mailboats' operations, their purpose was, of course, to transmit the mail on route 27098 under contract to the United States Post Office Department. In addition to the mail, other merchandise was accommodated separately as freight. Besides the riders' hand-carried personal items, there were occasionally other formal and informal

22

T. G. Winfield and bride-to-be Ludie Stall in 1919 in Linton

Courtesy of Will Ed Winfield

shipments - ranging from special orders to hidden containers of contraband goods.

The "sack" mail regularly consisted of at least one lockbag, containing the first-class mail, and an unlocked bag, holding the third and fourth-class mail, going to and from the post offices at Linton, Tobaccoport, and Dover. Other mail-dispatched cargo consisted of some larger packages sent by parcel post. These were carried by the boat operator from the landing directly to the town's post office - which, he hoped, was not too far from the dock. At the intermediate stop at Tobaccoport, this task was accomplished while the passengers waited aboard or near the landing.[125]

Eggs were regularly sent by mailboat. One driver, who insisted he carried no cargo apart from parcel post shipments, recalled that crates requiring such careful handling occupied a significant part of the boat's storage space near the front of the cabin's interior near the main doors.[126] Other parcel post items included furs, plows, plowpoints, harnesses, and, at least on one occasion, a saddle.[127]

If freight, apart from parcel post goods, was carried, one substitute driver recalled that it could not have been very significant since the passengers took up so much of the available space. What freight there was consisted mostly of catalog orders.[128] Another operator recalled kerosene being sent from Dover to stores in the area with at least two barrels stored outside along the narrow decking across the back of the boat.[129] Other items carried on different occasions included a wheel, a shotgun, and even a cooking stove.[130] One rider maintained that the mailboat regularly returned from Dover with goods for the stores of Tobaccoport and Linton.[131]

Passengers frequently brought aboard their own boxes (sacks were not then available) of groceries as they prepared to return to the landings near their home in more isolated areas of the valley.[132]

Copies of one of the regional newspapers, *The Nashville Banner,* were shipped in a bundle, transferred from the Cumberland City mailboat at Dover to the Linton mailboat for delivery to Tobaccoport.[133] At least one incident was recalled in which the driver of the Linton mailboat traded a newspaper for enough coal to fuel the cabin's stove.[134]

Some items, such as medicine, were picked up and delivered by drivers upon request.[135] Another example of such service was described by a Linton resident:

> I remember one time in high school in 1932, [two boys] caught the
> itch, the school got full of it, . . . we sent on the mailboat and got some
> salve from Dover and . . . met the boat to get it.[136]

Another contemporary remembered instances of illegal shipments on the mailboat. He claimed that some drivers "hauled a little white whiskey, out of sight."[137]

POST OFFICE OPERATIONS

The post offices in the three river towns obviously played an important role in the mailboat service on route 27098. The postmasters in these towns had duties similar to their counterparts in other towns across the country at the time, but in some ways, however, their mailboat responsibilities made their experiences somewhat different.

At Linton and Tobaccoport the postmasters always had to be on duty to prepare the mail shipments for early dispatch to Dover. They not only had to remain open until late in the afternoon for the return of the mailboat, but also had to be available to return and unlock the post office whenever the boat was delayed - sometimes as late as eleven o'clock at night.[138]

The postmaster normally had his office area in one of the town's general stores which he usually owned and operated while performing his duties. He would purchase eggs from suppliers, mark up the price for a profit from resale to buyers at destinations upstream, and then ship them out in crates subject to parcel post charges. The postmaster, who received no salary, thus made his postal earnings from the profits on the egg sales and the parcel post stamp cancellations from their shipment levies which he got to keep. In addition, of course, he received the proceeds from the sale of stamps and postal cards as well as for other items shipped by parcel post.[139] At one time during this period the Linton postmaster received two dollars in parcel post charges for each crate of his own eggs he shipped to Dover.[140] In addition, postage for each letter brought in one and one-half cents then. It was estimated that the Linton post office averaged about a dollar and a half a day.[141] If this figure is accurate, then egg shipments did not go out daily. In any case, the day's proceeds also included the sale of money orders.[142]

At times the combined duties of being both postmaster and store operator may have been too much - or perhaps the official was not too efficient or conscientious. One such official was remembered in the following account:

> One postmaster in [one of the towns], who will be nameless, let postcards pile up in the post office. The postal inspector came and asked why all those cards had accumulated. The postmaster said he had not had a chance to read them yet.[143]

FACILITIES AND CONDITIONS AT THE LANDINGS

Compared to modern riverfront accommodations for passenger and freight handling, the small landings along this stretch of the Cumberland were simple, if not primitive - but were apparently typical for their time. Even in the three towns there were no shoreline buildings in which passengers could wait or in which cargo could be stored.

Not only did the mailboats have no running or landing lights, but the landings themselves offered no illumination for arrivals and departures. Mention was made previously of lanterns aboard the craft which were used only as signals or warning lights when steamboats were encountered. On very dark or foggy evenings when the boat was late in returning, lanterns were sometimes posted at larger landings to direct the vessel to a safe landing.[144] One frequent rider recalled passengers carrying along their own lanterns during the darker part of the year so they could watch for cottonmouths when leaving the mailboat.[145] At Linton the landing was laid with cobblestone. Wagons could come down and turn around on the solid surface sloping to the river's edge. The mailboat was tied to a stob.[146]

Towboats carried ties from the Linton landing.[147] Drift pens were built at the river's edge to hold animals awaiting shipment on the steamboats which still called at least during the earlier years of this period. According to one source, the mailboat at one time was tied directly to the ferry which was fastened to the Linton landing. When the river was on the rise, men would stay up all night to move the drift pens up the slope and raise the tie-down fastenings of the boats.[148]

Tobaccoport had "just a hole in the bank" for its landing.[149] One rider, not entirely certain of his memory, believed there might have been a bell at that landing to signal the mailboat if a passenger wished to board when the vessel was not pulling in for mail delivery or pickup.[150] No one else mentioned such a practice.

As described previously, Dover had both upper and lower landings. Transfers occurred for passengers and mail between the two mailboats during the years both were in operation. In addition to being Dover's post office, the Joe Martin Company, a thriving equipment business, had an important tie with the Linton mailboat. The firm provided implements shipped to many land owners along this stretch of the river.[151]

The mailboat secured some if not all of its fuel at its Dover landing. A local oil dealer delivered gasoline to the landing where it was placed in a barrel set on the front of the boat.[152] In Dover passengers waiting for the mailboat to leave were able to stay in the relatively comfortable shelter provided by the garage of a local automobile dealer.[153] This must have been appreciated by passengers during periods of unfavorable weather.

AN UNEXPECTED CLOSING

The mailboat contract awarded to Millard Cherry in 1932 was to have extended through the four-year period until June 30, 1936. Even though automobiles were becoming more widely used and rural roads were being extended and improved within the region, the abrupt order of the Post Office Department affecting route 27098 issued on June 23, 1934, must have come as a surprise. With only seven days notice, the service on this route was to be terminated.[154] Gone would be not only the postal operation but also the passenger service of the Linton mailboat which had so long served the needs of these residents.

On that eventful day of June 30, 1934, the Linton mailboat made its last run to Dover and back - apparently without any fanfare or special ceremony. Thereafter all mail dispatches to and from Linton were routed entirely by land through Cadiz, the county seat.[155] The mail to and from Tobaccoport moved inland from the river through Bumpus Mills to Dover.[156] Power boat service on route 27098 had been discontinued. An era had come to an end.

Endnotes

1. Byrd Douglas, *Steamboatin' on the Cumberland* (Nashville: Tennessee Book Company, 1961), p. 224.

2. *Ibid.*, p. 259.

3. *Ibid.*, p. 261.

4. *Ibid.*, p. 285.

5. U.S. Post Office Department *Annual Report of the Postmaster General for the Fiscal Year Ended June 30, 1924*, in *Annual Reports 1921-1926* (Washington, D.C.: Government Printing Office, 1924), p. 22.

6. William Henry Perrin, ed., *Counties of Christian and Trigg, Kentucky* (Louisville and Chicago: F.A. Battey Publishing Company, 1884), p. 117.

7. Ellis B. Tucker, Linton, Kentucky, December 24, 1980. The entry in these notes of a name, location, and date indicates an interview.

8. Lillian Dawson, Linton, May 18, 1980. Mrs. Dawson spent her childhood years in Tobaccoport and now resides in Linton, where she writes a column entitled "From the Lakelands with Lillian" which regularly appears in the county's weekly newspaper, the *Cadiz Record*. It was this lady's reminiscences of the excitement and importance of the mailboat's arrival during her early years in Tobaccoport, which she described in on of her columns, that aroused my curiosity and interest and led me to undertake the study.

9. Charles Feltner, Cadiz, Kentucky, August 21, 1981.

10. B.W. Shelton, Tobaccoport, Tennessee, August 20, 1981; Geographical Site Location Report submitted by George H. Carr, postmaster at Linton, on March 25, 1912, and contained in Record Group No. 28, Series 187, United States Post Office Department, National Archives, Washington, D.C.

11. Lurline Moore, Cadiz, December 24, 1980. She maintained that the star route continued to operate throughout the period of mailboat service to Dover.

12. *Ibid.* This possibility or likelihood was also based upon conclusions drawn from mail routes shown for Trigg County prepared under the supervision of Richard N. Bird in the publication *General Scheme of Kentucky 1924*, U.S. Post Office Department (Washington, D.C.: Government Printing Office, 1924), p. 160. Further assumptions were made from correspondence with the National Archives, Washington, D.C.

13. Ellis B. Tucker, Linton, December 24, 1980.

14. *Stewart County Tennessee, Stewart County Heritage,* I (Dover, Tennessee: The Stewart County Historical Society, 1980), p. 15. "Upriver" is south because the Cumberland flows northward.

15. Bart Futrell, Linton, May 18, 1980.

16. *Ibid.*

17. J. Milton Henry, *The Land Between the Rivers* (n.p.: Taylor Publishing Company, n.d.), p. 27, citing *Stewart County Times,* October 21 and November 4, 1927, and March 23, 1928. Newspaper office file copies were destroyed by fire.

18. Gilbert Moore, Hopkinsville, Kentucky, August 21, 1981.

19. Charles Feltner, Cadiz, August 21, 1981.

20. Jerry N. Hess, Industrial and Social Branch, Civil Archives Division, National Archives, to author, July 14, 1980, accompanied by copies of contracts for the Steamboat Mail Service for Route 27098, Linton by Tobaccoport, to Dover, along with copies of all extant site location reports for these three post offices.

21. Ellis B. Tucker, Linton, May 18, 1980: Gray Acree, Sarasota, Florida, to author, April 3, 1981; Phil Peppers, Dover, Tennessee, May 19, 1980; Jack Nunn, Cadiz, May 18, 1980; Lillian Dawson, Linton, May 18, 1980. Additional evidence of this mailboat operation existing in that decade came from recollections of that period in Gray Acree's letter and from interviews with Lena Ezell, Hopkinsville, August 21, 1981, and Will Ed Winfield, Paducah, August 19, 1981, along with correspondence with the latter, December 7, 1981. Details of these accounts appear later.

22. *Contract for Steamboat Mail Service,* April 13, 1920, in Record Group No. 28, Power Boat registers, 1920-44, Tennessee-Kentucky Box 1, United States Post Office Department, located in the National Archives.

23. A compilation based on information gained from interviews with James H. Williams, Trigg County, Kentucky, May 18, 1980; Bill McNichols, Cadiz, May 18, 1980; Irene Ahart, Stewart County, Tennessee, May 19, 1980; Dan Dill, Dover, May 19, 1980; Bertha Edmunds, Dover, August 18, 1981; Clarence Cherry, Buchanan, Tennessee, August 18, 1981; Lillian Dawson, Linton, May 18, 1980; Gilbert Moore, Hopkinsville, August 21, 1981; and Lena Ezell, Hopkinsville, August 21, 1981; a letter and a simple hand-drawn sketch map contributed by Gray Acree, Sarasota, Florida, April 3, 1981; and landings identified on maps in the figures contained in this article.

24. Bertha Edmunds, Dover, August 18, 1981.

25. Clarence Cherry, Buchanan, Tennessee, August 18, 1981.

26. *Ibid.*

27. Mack Hester, Dover, August 18, 1981; Clarence Cherry, Buchanan, August 18, 1981.

28. G. C. Graham, Symsonia, Kentucky, August 19, 1981.

29. Cecil Gibbs, Dover, August 18, 1981.

30. Bertha Edmunds, Dover, August 18, 1981.

31. James H. Williams, Trigg County, May 18, 1980.

32. For date of completion of Lock D, see *Stewart County, Tennessee,* p. 16; Bill McNichols, Cadiz, May 18, 1980.

33. Lurline Moore, Cadiz, December 24, 1980.

34. Clarence Cherry, Buchanan, August 18, 1981.

35. *General Advertisement of Oct. 27, 1931* (for Route 27098 showing statement of route of schedule), Record Group No. 28, Power Boat Service, Second

Contract Section, 1932-1945, United States Post Office Department, located in the National Archives.

36. Richard N. Bird, *General Scheme of Kentucky*, p. 160.

37. Bill McNichols, Cadiz, May 18, 1980.

38. James H. Williams, Trigg County, May 18, 1980.

39. Bill McNichols, Cadiz, May 18, 1980.

40. Helen Bartter Crocker, *The Green River of Kentucky* (Lexington: University Press of Kentucky, 1976), pp. 54-55.

41. Bill McNichols, Cadiz, May 18, 1980.

42. *Ibid.*

43. James H. Williams, Trigg County, May 18, 1980.

44. Gilbert Moore, Hopkinsville, August 21, 1981.

45. Bill McNichols, Cadiz, May 18, 1980.

46. Gray Acree to author, April 3, 1981.

47. James H. Williams, Trigg County, May 18, 1980.

48. *Contract for Steamboat Mail Service* for Route 27098, four successive, four-year, low-bid awards dated April 13, 1920, February 15, 1924, February 9, 1928, and February 24, 1932, in Record Group No. 28, Power Boat Registers 1920-44, Tennessee-Kentucky Box 1, United States Post Office Department, located in the National Archives, Washington, D.C.

49. Bill McNichols, Cadiz, May 18, 1980; James H. Williams, Trigg County, May 18, 1980; and Lena Ezell, Hopkinsville, August 21, 1981; letters from Weaks Martin, Kerrville, Texas, June 4, 1980; and Will Ed Winfield, Paducah, December 7, 1981; Bart Futrell, Linton, May 18, 1980.

50. Lillian Dawson, Linton, May 18, 1980; Lena Ezell, Hopkinsville, August 31, 1981; Bart Futrell, Linton, May 18, 1980; Perry Greenhill, Dover, May 19, 1980; G. C. Graham, Symsonia, August 19, 1981; Bill McNichols, Cadiz, May 18, 1980; Gilbert Moore, Hopkinsville, August 21, 1981; Lurline Moore, Cadiz, December 24, 1980; Jack Nunn, Cadiz, May 18, 1980; James H. Williams, Trigg County, May 18, 1980; and information secured by phone from Erwin Winfield, Linton, May 18, 1980, and relayed by Jack Nunn during interview. Recollections of the identity of others who drove mailboats during this era were subject to some uncertainty because of confusion in distinguishing between builders and owners, regular and substitute drivers, and persons active on the Linton-Dover and those on the Dover-Cumberland City routes.

51. James H. Williams, Trigg County, may 18, 1980; Bill McNichols, Cadiz, May 18, 1980.

52. *Ibid.*

53. Will Ed Winfield, Paducah, to author, December 7, 1981.

54. Clarence Cherry, Buchanan, Tennessee, August 18, 1981.

55. *Ibid.*

56. B. W. Shelton, Tobaccoport, August 20, 1981; Gray Acree, Sarasota, Florida, to author, April 3, 1981.

57. Ellis B. Tucker, Linton, August 20, 1981.

58. Clarence Cherry, Buchanan, August 18, 1981.

59. Bart Futrell, Linton, May 18, 1980, and Bill McNichols, Cadiz, May 18, 1980; Will Ed Winfield, Paducah, to author, December 7, 1981, and Gray Acree, Sarasota, Florida, to author, April 3, 1981.

60. B. W. Shelton, Tobaccoport, August 20, 1981.

61. Gilbert Moore, Hopkinsville, August 21, 1981.

62. Clarence Cherry, Buchanan, August 18, 1981.

63. Gilbert Moore, Hopkinsville, August 21, 1981.

64. *Ibid.;* B. W. Shelton, Tobaccoport, August 20, 1981.

65. Gilbert Moore, Hopkinsville, August 21, 1981.

66. Bart Futrell, Linton, May 18, 1980; Lillian Dawson, Linton, May 18, 1980; Cecil Gibbs, Dover, August 18, 1981; and Mack Hester, Dover, August 18, 1981; Will Ed Winfield, Paducah, to author, December 7, 1981; Gilbert Moore, Hopkinsville, August 21, 1981; and Clarence Cherry, Buchanan, August 18, 1981; Lurline Moore, Cadiz, December 24, 1980.

67. Cecil Gibbs, Dover, August 18, 1981.

68. Bill McNichols, Cadiz, May 18, 1980.

69. Charles Feltner, Cadiz, August 21, 1981; G. C. Graham, Symsonia, August 19, 1981; James H. Williams, Trigg County, May 18, 1980; Gilbert Moore, Hopkinsville, August 21, 1981; Clarence Cherry, Buchanan, August 18, 1981.

70. Gilbert Moore, Hopkinsville, August 21, 1981; B. W. Shelton, Tobaccoport, August 20, 1981.

71. Gilbert Moore, Hopkinsville, August 21, 1981.

72. B. W. Shelton, Tobaccoport, August 20, 1981.

73. Clarence Cherry, Buchanan, August 18, 1981; Charles Feltner, Cadiz, August 21, 1981; Cecil Gibbs, Dover, August 18, 1981; G. C. Graham, Symsonia, August 19, 1981.

74. Charles Feltner, Cadiz, August 21, 1981.

75. G. C. Graham, Symsonia, August 19, 1981.

76. Weaks Martin, Kerrville, Texas, to author, June 4, 1980; Bart Futrell, Linton, May 18, 1980; Bill McNichols, Cadiz, May 18, 1980; James H. Williams, Trigg County, May 18, 1980.

77. Clarence Cherry, Buchanan, August 18, 1981.

78. Gilbert Moore, Hopkinsville, August 21, 1981.

79. B. W. Shelton, Tobaccoport, August 20, 1981.

80. Lena Ezell, Hopkinsville, August 21, 1981.

81. James H. Williams, Trigg County, May 18, 1980.

82. G. C. Graham, Symsonia, August 19, 1981.

83. Gilbert Moore, Hopkinsville, August 21, 1981.

84. Bart Futrell, Linton, May 18, 1980; Lena Ezell, Hopkinsville, August 21, 1981.

85. Bill McNichols, Cadiz, May 18, 1980.

86. *Ibid.*

87. G. C. Graham, Symsonia, August 19, 1981.

88. Lena Ezell, Hopkinsville, August 21, 1981.

89. B. W. Shelton, Tobaccoport, August 20, 1981.

90. Clarence Cherry, Buchanan, August 18, 1981.

91. Gilbert Moore, Hopkinsville, August 21, 1981.

92. B. W. Shelton, Tobaccoport, August 20, 1981.

93. G. C. Graham, Symsonia, August 19, 1981; Will Ed Winfield, Paducah, August 19, 1981.

94. G. C. Graham, Symsonia, August 19, 1981.

95. Clarence Cherry, Buchanan, August 18, 1981.

96. Will Ed Winfield, Paducah, August 19, 1981.

97. Lena Ezell, Hopkinsville, August 21, 1981.

98. Clarence Cherry, Buchanan, August 18, 1981; Bart Futrell, Linton, May 18, 1980.

99. Clarence Cherry, Buchanan, August 18, 1981.

100. James H. Williams, Trigg County, May 18, 1980.

101. Bill McNichols and Jack Nunn, Cadiz, May 18, 1980; Charles Feltner, Cadiz, August 21, 1981.

102. Bertha Edmunds, Dover, August 18, 1981.

103. James H. Williams, Trigg County, May 18, 1980; Charles Feltner, Cadiz, August 21, 1981; G. C. Graham, Symsonia, August 19, 1981.

104. Bill McNichols, Cadiz, May 18, 1980.

105. Charles Feltner, Cadiz, August 21, 1981.

106. *Ibid.*

107. Mrs. Jake Hunter, Cadiz, to author, June 17, 1980.

108. Charles Feltner, Cadiz, August 21, 1981.

109. Lurline Moore, Cadiz, December 24, 1980.

110. Will Ed Winfield, Paducah, August 19, 1981.

111. Gilbert Moore, Hopkinsville, August 21, 1981.

112. Ellis B. Tucker, Linton, August 20, 1981.

113. Gray Acree, Sarasota, Florida, to author, April 3, 1981.

114. Clarence Cherry, Buchanan, August 18, 1981.

115. Gilbert Moore, Hopkinsville, August 21, 1981.

116. Bertha Edmunds, Dover, August 18, 1981.

117. James H. Williams, Trigg County, May 18, 1980.

118. *Ibid.*

119. Jack Nunn, Cadiz, May 18, 1980.

120. Lena Ezell, Hopkinsville, August 21, 1981.

121. Bill McNichols, Cadiz, May 18, 1980.

122. Lena Ezell, Hopkinsville, August 21, 1981.

123. Will Ed Winfield, Paducah, to author, December 7, 1981.

124. Gilbert Moore, Hopkinsville, August 21, 1981.

125. Bart Futrell, Linton, May 18, 1980; Clarence Cherry, Buchanan, August 18, 1981.

126. James H. Williams, Trigg County, may 18, 1980.

127. N. W. Carr, Linton, May 19, 1980; G. C. Graham, Symsonia, August 19, 1981; Gilbert Moore, Hopkinsville, August 21, 1981; James H. Williams, Trigg County, May 18, 1980.

128. Gilbert Moore, Hopkinsville, August 21, 1981.

129. Clarence Cherry, Buchanan, August 18, 1981.

130. Charles Feltner, Cadiz, August 21, 1981; B. W. Shelton, Tobaccoport, August 20, 1981.

131. Lillian Dawson, Linton, May 18, 1980.

132. B. W. Shelton, Tobaccoport, August 20, 1981.

133. *Ibid.*

134. James H. Williams, Trigg County, May 18, 1980.

135. Bertha Edmunds, Dover, August 18, 1981.

136. Bill McNichols, Cadiz, May 18, 1980.

137. Cecil Gibbs, Dover, August 18, 1981.

138. Bill McNichols, Cadiz, May 18, 1980.

139. James H. Williams, Trigg County, May 18, 1980; Bill McNichols and Jack Nunn, Cadiz, May 18, 1980.

140. Bill McNichols, Cadiz, May 18, 1980.

141. Jack Nunn, Cadiz, May 18, 1980.

142. N. W. Carr, Linton, May 19, 1980.

143. Jack Nunn, Cadiz, May 18, 1980.

144. Will Ed Winfield, Paducah, August 19, 1981.

145. Bertha Edmunds, Dover, August 18, 1981.

146. G. C. Graham, Symsonia, August 19, 1981.

147. Charles Feltner, Cadiz, August 21, 1981.

148. G. C. Graham, Symsonia, August 19, 1981.

149. *Ibid.*

150. Charles Feltner, Cadiz, August 21, 1981.

151. *Ibid.*

152. G. C. Graham, Symsonia, August 19, 1981.

153. *Ibid.*

154. Order, June 23, 1934, signed by J. M. Donaldson, Acting Second Assistant Postmaster General, in Record Group No. 28, Power Boat service, Second Contract Section, 1932-1945, United States Post Office Department, located in the National Archives. The communique read: "From June 30, 1934, discontinue service, and allow contractor one month's extra pay."

155. James H. Williams, Trigg County, May 18, 1980, later documented by a communication response from E. Perkins Carr, Postmaster at Linton, dated August 19, 1940, in Record Group No. 28, Series 187, Geographical Site Location Report, United States Post Office Department, located in the National Archives.

156. James H. Williams, Trigg County, May 18, 1980, later documented by a communication response from W. D. Scarborough, Postmaster at Tobaccoport, dated October 20, 1937, in Record Group No. 28, Series 187, Geographical Site Location Report, United States Post Office Department, located in the National Archives.

"Wolf Island: From a Haven for River Pirates to an Assignment for a Ferryboat-Commuting Schoolteacher" is a previously unpublished manuscript by the author of this book.

Permission to include content contained in this chapter, as credited in the footnote entries and beneath the photo illustrations, was generously granted by the sources indicated below.

The Courier-Journal, Louisville, Kentucky

Lawyers Co-operative Publishing Company, Rochester, New York

The Mayfield Messenger, Mayfield, Kentucky

Mr. John S. Osborn, Jr., attorney, Louisville, Kentucky

The Paducah Sun, Paducah, Kentucky

2

WOLF ISLAND, KENTUCKY

*Wolf Island: From A Haven For River
Pirates To An Assignment For A Ferryboat-
Commuting Schoolteacher*

On the Missouri side of the Mississippi River, about twenty miles downstream from the point at which this great artery is joined by the Ohio River, lies the area known as Wolf Island (Fig. 1). This survivor of more eventful days, still a part politically of Hickman County in the Jackson Purchase section of western Kentucky, today appears to be in the final stage of becoming physically attached to the mainland of Mississippi County across the river in the neighboring state. With the nearly completed obliteration of the remnants of the earlier slough along its inland side, Wolf Island now is a misnomer for this once-historic isle also shown on navigation maps of the past as Island No. 5.

E.D. White, who during this century owned property on Wolf Island, accounted for the area's origin as he perceived it in the following excerpt taken from a more lengthy description of the island's history:

> In the early dawn of long, long ago a great quagmire of swamp land many miles wide existed west of Columbus. The Gulf of Mexico had retreated southward from Cairo and had left the swamp with many running bayous and no clear cut river channel.
>
> During this very early period in our geological life, great winds from the barren western lands covered this area with dust, the like of which we have never seen. Millions upon millions of tons were deposited here like snow drifts.
>
> Perhaps the humidity of the great swamp caused the dust to fall. It created the high bluffs at Columbus and elsewhere up and down the river in Hickman County. Soil formed from these deep dust deposits was very fertile and is called "loess."
>
> Floods through the "Great Swamp" running bayous gradually build up islands and in other places created depressions in lakes. In this way Wolf Island was formed. The drainage finally became established in one stream and became a river, the Mississippi. Wolf Island was high land in the middle. The river then was perhaps as large, or even larger, on the Missouri side as on the Kentucky side.[1]

During the late 1700's and into the first few years of the 1800's Wolf Island gained a reputation as a haven for river pirates. The most noted desperado was Samuel Mason who used this island hideout to direct the undertakings of one of the largest groups "of murderers and cutthroats that had ever been assembled."[2] Mason, who reportedly had established a creditable military record

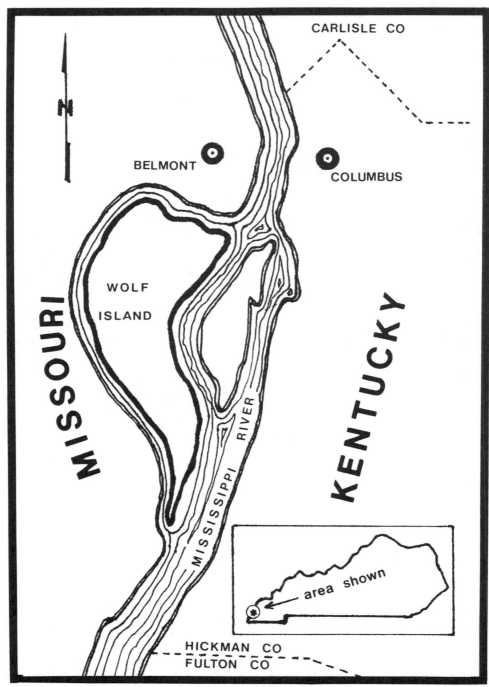

Fig. 1 - Setting for Wolf Island

Map by Brent Parsons

36

while serving with General George Rogers Clark's "Longknives" during their trip downriver to old Fort Massac and subsequent expedition to capture Vincennes, had later first settled in the Kentucky community of Red Banks (afterwards to become Henderson) along the Ohio River where he joined his first gang of robbers operating from nearby Diamond Island while serving as the local justice of peace and protecting his comrades whenever they were brought before his court.[3]

When Mason's daughter entered into an unwelcomed marriage with one of the Diamond Island ruffians and his new son-in-law was found murdered outside his father-in-law's cabin under rather suspicious circumstances following a "healing celebration" of the family rift, Mason and his sons hurriedly departed Red Banks for the infamous Cave-in-Rock hideout downstream on the Illinois side. A threat of an imminent attack from a fleet of ships coming from Pittsburg to eradicate this pirate hideaway led to a hasty division of the personnel of the haven. Mason and his recruits headed for Wolf Island as a new base for operations, which included the rather distant Natchez Trace.[4] This new location "furnished an excellent hideout for Mason. The island is in Kentucky. Across the river was Spanish territory. On the Spanish side he posed as a respected citizen. In Kentucky and in Mississippi he was hunted like a wild animal."[5]

Eventually he was captured and taken to New Madrid for trial early in 1803. While the Spanish officials deliberated whether he should stand trial in their territory or be turned over to the "frontier justice" of Kentucky or Mississippi, Mason solved their problem by escaping with his band and taking to the wild for a number of months before he was executed for "the price on his head" and subsequently "ended up with his severed head encased in a ball of blue Mississippi swamp mud."[6]

The main channel of the Mississippi River until about this time apparently passed on the west side of Wolf Island, a comparatively large island in the region during this period of history. When Missouri entered the Union in 1820, the state assumed its eastern boundary to be set by the middle of the Mississippi River channel, but later maintained that this channel actually should have been recognized as lying east of Wolf Island at the time of admission.

But if it is true that the main channel of the river actually did lie along the west side of the island when Missouri entered the Union, then it seems that "between 1820 and 1870, the river channel began to shift toward Kentucky and the Missouri chute began to silt in."[7]

The State of Missouri in 1859 initiated proceedings against the State of Kentucky in the Supreme Court of the United States to secure a court decree which would establish the legal boundary between the two states and "determine officially the ownership of Wolf Island."[8] The case was eventually argued and decided in 1871. Mr. Justice Davis, in delivering the opinion of the court, weighed carefully the contentions of the opposing parties:

> That Virginia claimed the ownership of the island as early as 1782 is very certain, for at that date the arable land on it was entered in the proper office of Virginia as vacant land lying within the territorial limits of the state, 402*] although it *seems the entry was never sur-

veyed or carried into a grant. And that Kentucky is now, and has been for many years prior to the commencement of this suit, in the actual and exclusive possession of the island, exercising the rights of sovereignty over it, is beyond dispute. The island lies opposite to and forms part of Hickman county, one of the counties of the state, and the lands embraced in it were, in May, 1837, surveyed under state authority, and have since then been sold and conveyed to the purchasers by the same authority. The people residing on it have paid taxes and exercised the elected franchise according to the laws of the state. In 1851, a resident of the island was elected to represent the county in the general assembly, and served in that capacity. And as early as 1828, a minor living there with one Samuel Scott, was bound an apprentice to him by the proper court having jurisdiction of such subjects. This possession, fully established by acts like these, has never been disturbed. If Missouri has claimed the island to be within her boundaries, she has made no attempt to subject the people living there to her laws, or to require of them the performance of any duty belonging to the citizens of a state. Nor has there been any effort on her part to occupy the island, or to exercise jurisdiction over it. If there were proof that the island, by legislation, had been included in the limits of New Madrid county, then the service of a writ in 1820, on the solitary settler there, by the sheriff of the county, would be an exercise of sovereign power on the part of the state. But in the absence of this proof, there is nothing to connect the state with the transaction, or from which an inference can be drawn that the sheriff was authorized to go on the island with his process. And for the same reason, it is hard to see how the fact, conceding it to be true, that a person occupying the position of a circuit judge of Missouri, once lived on the island (when or how long we are not informed), tends to show that the state intended to take possession of it.[9]

The evidence that was considered in the case consisted of "the testimony of living witnesses, the physical changes and indications at and above the island, and the maps and books produced by the complainant."[10] Since the detailed recollections of some witnesses and other extensive information is of considerable interest in revealing the early history and physical changes during this era on Wolf Island, an unusually lengthy extract is taken from the original proof:

There are eight witnesses called for the complainant, who testify confidently, that the main channel of the Mississippi river was always east of Wolf island, and one of them (Swon), an experienced river man, who navigated the river from 1821 to 1851, in all stages of water, says there are no indications that the main channel was ever on the west side. Only three of them knew the river prior to 1820, and they were engaged in business of flat boating, which is hardly ever undertaken in a low stage of water. There is nothing to show that any one of them ever made a personal examination of the channels and surrounding objects at this point, and there is a remarkable absence of facts to sustain their opinions. It is also noticeable, in connection with this evidence, that none of the witnesses (Hunter may be an exception) *ever lived in the vicinity of [*404] the island, or remained there any length of time, and that all the knowledge any of them acquired of the state of the river was obtained by passing up or down it at different times, either on flat-boats or steamboats. Notwithstanding they swear positively that the channel was always east of the island, yet Watson says it changed for about three years, and Ranney testifies that on one occasion, when the main channel was divided into three parts, the deepest water for a short time in the fall of the year was found on the west of the island, and steamboats passed on that side. But they do not prove a deficiency of water at any time in the Missouri channel, or that any boat, from that or any other cause, was ever hindered in any attempt to run it. It is un-doubtedly true that the Kentucky channel, when the river was full, for many years has afforded a safe passage for boats, because at such a time, if the obstructions were not submerged they could be avoided, and navigators would take it, as it was five miles the shortest. And passing the river only occasionally, and without any knowledge of where the volume of water flowed when the river was low, they would naturally conclude it was the main channel. It is equally true that now it is the main highway for the business of the river. . .

The proof on behalf of the defendant consists of the testimony of twenty-seven witnesses. Many of them have been acquainted with the river from an early period in this century, and quite a number have spent their lives near their disputed territory and, therefore, had better opportunities for observing the condition of the river at this point than the witnesses for the complainant, who only passed there occasionally. Nearly all of them are old men, and there is no diversity of opinion between them concerning the location [405*] *of the main channel of the Mississippi river at Wolf island. All who testify on the subject -- there are only a few who do not -- agree that until a comparatively recent period it ran west of the island, and to fortify their opinions they describe the state of the respective channel at different times, and tell what was done by themselves or others about the navigation of the river. They concur in saying that in early times it was difficult for flat-boats, even in the highest stage of water, to get into the Kentucky chute, owing to the current running towards the Missouri side, and that if they succeeded in doing it, the navigation was obstructed on account of the narrow and crooked condition of the stream, which was filled with tow-heads, sandbars, driftwood, and rack heaps. One of the witnesses, in describing the appearance of this chute in 1804, states that it looked like lowlands, with cottonwood and cypress on it, and that there was only a narrow channel close to the island; all the other space to the Kentucky shore, now open water, was then covered with large cottonwood timber.

Other witnesses corroborate this testimony, and unite in saying that in early times, at an ordinary stage of water, it was impossible to take the Kentucky channel at all, on account of these obstructions, while the Missouri channel was wide, deep and unobstructed. And one of them expresses the opinion that in low water anyone could have got to the island from the Kentucky shore without wetting his feet, by crossing the small streams on the driftwood. But we are not left to conjecture on this point, for Ramsey, an old inhabitant of the country, swears that on one occasion he walked over from the Kentucky side to the island, nearly all the way on dry land, and the residue on driftwood, and noticed while on the island, that there was plenty of water in the Missouri channel.

Can it be possible that such a stream at this time was the main channel of the Mississippi river? Although the Kentucky channel, from natural causes, had improved in 1825, still in the low water of that year it did not have a depth of over two and a half feet nor a width [406*] exceeding one hundred *and fifty yards, while steamboats passed through the Missouri channel without any difficulty. The witness who testifies to this state of things, at that time, had his attention especially called to the subject as he kept a woodyard on the Kentucky side opposite the island, and missed the opportunity of supplying boats that ran the Missouri channel.

And there is no one who speaks of a scarcity of water in the Missouri channel, until after Captain Shreve operated in this locality with his snag boats, which had the effect of opening and deepening the Kentucky channel, so that it has now become the navigable stream. Judge Underwood says that in 1820 the west channel was between four and five hundred yards wider than the east one, and must have discharged nearly double the quantity of water. And one witness testifies that the east channel was formerly so narrow that two steamers could not pass in it abreast. It would seem therefore, that the condition of this channel, as told by these witnesses, was proof enough that the main channel was west of the island; but this is not all the proof on the subject. Russell, who was appointed superintendent of river improvements in 1842, and knew the island since 1814, and spent five months there in 1819, swears that in descending the river in 1830 or 1831 he sounded the Kentucky channel and, not finding water enough in it by two or three feet to float his boat, was compelled to go down on the Missouri side, where there was nine or ten feet of water. To the same effect is the evidence of Holton, who, in 1828, being unable to get up the east channel with a steamer drawing upwards of six feet of water, went over to the Missouri side and passed through without any trouble. And, three years later, Peebles saw three or four steamers attempt to run up the Kentucky channel, and failing to get through, back out and easily ascend the other. Christopher, who ran the river from 1824 to 1861, on one occasion could not pass the bar at the foot of the Kentucky chute with a boat drawing twelve feet of water, and was compelled to change to the other side, and got up without any difficulty; and there are other witnesses who testify to the inability of boats to *pass east of the island, and to their [*407] safe passage west of it. Indeed, the concurrent testimony of all the persons engaged in the navigation of the river is, that they could never safely go east of the island, unless in high water, and that they uniformly took the west channel in dry seasons; and the flat-boat men, in early times, even in high water, were frequently compelled to uncouple their boats in order to descend the Kentucky channel, and then were obliged to pull through by trees, on account of the narrowness of the channel. In low water they would quite often get aground and have to wait for a rise of the river to take them out. It will readily be seen that this class of men would naturally take risks in order to save five miles of navigation. Moseby, who has lived in the vicinity for forty-two years, testifies to the greater volume of water in the Missouri channel, and to boats usually taking it; and all the witnesses agree that since they knew the river the chutes around the island have undergone great changes, and that the east one is now, in depth, width and freedom from obstructions, wholly unlike what it was formerly. In this state of proof, how can it be successfully contended that Missouri has any claim to the island?

But there is additional proof growing out of certain physical facts connected with this locality which we will proceed to consider. Islands are formed in the Mississippi river by accretions produced by the deposit at a particular place of the soil and sand constantly floating in it, and by the river cutting a new channel through the mainland on one or the other of its shores. The inquiry naturally suggests itself: of which class is Wolf island? If the latter, then the further inquiry whether it was detached from Missouri or Kentucky. The evidence applicable to this subject tends strongly to show that the island is not the result of accretions, but was once a part of the mainland of Kentucky. Islands formed by accretions are, in river phraseology, called made land, while those produced by the other process necessarily are of primitive formation. It is easy to distinguish them on account of the difference in their soil and timber.

408*] *It has been found by observation and experience that primitive soil produces trees chiefly of the hard wood varieties, while the timber growing on land of secondary formation -- the effect of accretions -- is principally cottonwood. Wolf island is of large area, containing about fifteen thousand acres of land, and, with the exception of some narrow accretions on its shore, is primitive land, and has the primitive forest growing on it.

On the high land of the island there are the largest poplar, chinquapin, oak and blackjack trees growing, and primitive soil only has the constituent elements to produce such timber. But this is not all, for trees of like kind and size are found on the Kentucky side, on what is called the second bottom, near the foot of the Iron Banks, which is about two feet higher than the bottom on which Columbus is located. There are no such trees on the Missouri shore. Those found there are of a different kind and much smaller growth. Besides this, the highland on the island is on the same level with the second bottom on the Kentucky side, while it is four or five feet higher than the land on the Missouri side opposite the island and above it. In this state of the case, it would seem clear that this second bottom and island were once parts of the same table of land and, at some remote period, were separated by the formation of the east channel. In the nature of things, it is impossible to tell when this occurred, nor is it necessary to decide that question, for, by the memory of living witnesses, we are enabled to determine that the east channel, or cut off, as it should be called, was not the main channel down to 1820.

If the testimony already noticed be not enough to prove this, there is the additional evidence furnished by the changes which the river has accomplished in the neighborhood of the island, within the recollection of many intelligent persons. These changes are important, and are shown on map [ante, 117], of H.G. Black, which is proved to be a correct representation both of the present and original position of the island, the river, and its banks. The effect of the evidence on this subject is, [410*] that the filling *up at the mouth of Town creek, the washing

41

away of the point above on the Missouri side, the abrasion of the Iron Banks, and the partial destruction of Toney's point, have operated to straighten the banks above the island on the Kentucky side, to bring the water closer to them and, as a consequence, to cast it into the east channel. And that before these projecting points were removed and the accretions made at Town creek, the water was thrown towards the Missouri side. This was necessarily so, as can readily be seen by an inspection of the map. In the original condition of the river, the current must have been carried from the Missouri point to the Iron Banks opposite, and rebounded from them across to the Missouri side, so as to carry the channel west of Wolf island. And it is equally clear that the changes which have occurred within this century have straightened the river and turned the channel to the east of the island. Can there be any need of further evidence to sustain the long-continued possession of Kentucky to the island, and are not the witnesses who swear that in their time the main channel of the Mississippi river ran west of Wolf island abundantly fortified?

But it is said the maps of the early explorers of the river and the reports of travelers prove the channel always to have been east of the island. The answer to this is, that evidence of this character is mere hearsay as to facts within the memory of witnesses, and if this consideration does not exclude all the books and maps since 1800, it certainly renders them of little value in the determination of the question in dispute. If such evidence differs from that of living witnesses based on facts, the latter is to be preferred. Can there be a doubt that it would be wrong in principle to dispossess a party of property on the mere statements -- not sworn to -- of travelers and explorers, when living witnesses, testifying under oath and subject to cross-examination, and the physical facts of the case, contradict them?

But it is claimed the books and maps which antedate human testimony establish the right of Missouri to this island. If this be so, there is recent authority for [*411] saying they are *unreliable. In 1861, Captain Humphreys and Lieutenant Abbott, of the corps of topographical engineers, submitted to the proper bureau of the War Department a report based on actual surveys and investigations, upon the physics and hydraulics of the Mississippi river, which they were directed to make by Congress. In speaking on the subject of the changes in the river (p. 104), they say: "These changes have been constantly going on since the settlement of the country, but the old maps and records are so defective that it is impossible to determine much about those which occurred prior to 1800." In the face of this report, authorized by the government and prepared with great learning and industry, how can we allow the books and maps published prior to this century to have any weight in the decision of this controversy?

Without pursuing the investigation further, on full consideration of all the evidence in the case, we are satisfied that the state of Missouri has no just claim to the possession of Wolf island.[11]

Although land on the island reportedly was transferred as a land grant to private ownership from federal control following the Revolutionary War,[12] another source reports that veterans of the Civil War were the first recipients of lots granted on Wolf Island. Among those recorded as holders of title to such lots soon after the end of the war were the Baker, Cook, Edrington, and Stephen families.[13] Other early settlers were reported to have originated from Union County, Kentucky and after descending the Ohio River added the names of McConnell, Stanley, and Wright to the first residents of the isle. These last-named pioneers were described as having found that "the land was rich and a livelihood was easy to gain."[14] As time passed other families located on a growing Wolf Island.[15]

During the last half of the century the island was considered to be "somewhat inaccessible" due to the presence of navigable channels remaining on both sides of the isle at that time. But the island was of sufficient elevation that widespread flooding occurred only occasionally. Thus continuous occupance generally was possible.[16]

The local historian, E.D. White, is quoted in one article in reminiscing about the early days when "'most of the island was in timber and the people operated small farms'".[17] He further recalled that a steamboat landing was located about midway on the western side of the island where supplies were unloaded for the inhabitants.[18]

In his own account White indicated that Wolf Island once was reported to have contained about 17,000 acres. He felt, however, that the early estimate might have been too large.[19]

The first school on the island was opened in 1881 "in an old log house."[20] The enrollment in the school for white children averaged approximately fifteen during the years that followed. A separate school "for colored students was also maintained for many years."[21] Another investigator accounted for a one-room school established before 1926 that served the first eight grades, apparently for white children. Enrollment in this school, until the disruption of the flood of 1937, was estimated for each year as ranging "between fifty and sixty pupils."[22]

One writer reported that in 1913 "as many as 50 permanent families lived on the island, many of them prosperous and well-to-do farmers."[23] The population of the island began to decline gradually following the disastrous flood of that year.[24] Yet another article counted possibly 50 permanent families still on the isle at the close of the 1930's.[25]

Mrs. John Watts, who later served as the Fulton County school system's director of pupil personnel, recalled a Wolf Island "when it was a sizable community."[26] During 1935 and 1936 she was the teacher in the one-room school for the white children on the isle. To get to her school she boarded the ferry at Columbus to cross the river to the Missouri side where she rode "the rest of the way into the island by wagon, car or boat...."[27]

During the major floods of 1927 and 1937 the water of the Mississippi expanded, flowed over Wolf Island, and swept away the possessions of the residents. By 1941 the extent of these floods had "made Wolf Islanders a fearful lot."[28] The author who visited the island in early January of that unsettled year found "a group of humble, God-loving Kentuckians," numbering about 115, who resided on the lonely isle.[29] He described these occupants as gathered "about

43

Hard-packed roads connect island homes. Recent flood have taken away soil instead of adding it. Corn once grew 52 bushels an acre, but won't now. [1941]
C.-J. Photo by PENCE
Reprint from article photocopy as only available source
Permission of The Courier-Journal

the log fires in their cozy but unpretentious home," erected on stilts, where they contemplated what 1941 might bring to their disturbed world.[30]

The residents of that isolated island settlement had the advantages of such modern conveniences as the automobile and the radio and generally kept up rather well with the news of their time.[31]

While the remainder of the world was worried about the expanding war, one into which the United States would soon be drawn, and what might be its duration, the folks of this narrow island of about six miles length and two miles width were more occupied with what they regarded in their little corner of the world as "the most vital problem": the dilemma in which they continued to find themselves in regard to the unpredictable Mississippi River.[32]

A majority of the occupants of Wolf Island in 1941 has resided there for years, preceded by their fathers and grandfathers. They owned the small tracts which they farmed and had bought and paid for their property with the profits from the cotton, grain, and livestock which they had raised.[33]

But the effects of the recent ruinous floods had made these islanders uneasy. They readily conceded that life on the island had changed. Valuable pecan and walnut trees had disappeared after many acres of timber had been harvested.

The soil was not as fertile as it had been earlier. The latest floods had not deposited a new layer of alluvium, but instead had washed away much of the rich topsoil of the island. It appeared the local residents blamed outsiders from the mainland who had roles in the timber removal without having had regard for arrangements for provision of replacement seedlings and grass sowing to retain the soil cover. Such consequences, Wolf Islanders contended, were forcing them to relinquish their homes as their properties became less productive.[34] Old residents of the island believed that the population had been cut nearly in half by 1941 in the thirteen years since the first of the two major floods that had besieged their isle. They feared that if nothing was going to be done to help the soil retain water in the region, Wolf Island might be covered each year with renewed inundation and the occupants would be forced to abandon their homeland.[35]

After the 1927 flood the Mississippi began to change its course. Even by 1941 Wolf Island was becoming less of an island and more of an attachment to Missouri. Yet the responsibility of the residents to commute to Clinton, the county seat on the mainland of their Hickman County governing entity, to pay their county and state taxes annually seemed to reconfirm their status as Kentuckians.[36]

So in 1941 the earlier main channel on the Missouri side of the island was normally a dry channel nominally separating Wolf Island from the Missouri mainland. Occupants of the isle had constructed a road across the abandoned channel, which they labeled the Chute. The road then entered Missouri. Rather than using their own boats to cross the Mississippi to get to Columbus, the nearest town on the Kentucky mainland, Wolf Islanders now drove from their homes on their new road across the Chute into their recently-joined state of Missouri where only a short distance north at Belmont they could drive their cars aboard the ferry to Columbus with the road there leading them to Clinton and points beyond.[37]

The normally dry Chute in 1941 only filled with water "during the winter and spring rises" and at that time was only about 100 feet in width.[38]

Even though many of the island's occupants had fled to the mainland following the ravages of the floods, enough of the residents remained to justify the continuation of a school. In 1941 Miss Blanche Baker of Clinton taught twenty-one students distributed among the eight grades in the one-room building authorized by the Hickman County school board.[39]

John Irbey, then the oldest resident at 71 on Wolf Island, had lived there for fifty-two years. He was in 1941 the largest property owner on the remote isle where he lived with other members of his family. Writer Bosler captured the recollections of this old-timer:

> The old island just ain't what she used to be.... The floods won't let us alone. Time was when we lived happy and peaceful here; raised all we could eat, made enough money and enjoyed life. But now, well, you just don't know when the Mississippi will come up and wash you away. Most of the timber is gone and the land is not as good as it used to be. Back

Home of John Irbey, 71, the island's oldest inhabitant, stands on concrete pilings. He has been a Wolf Islander for fifty-two years. [1941]
Reprint from article photocopy as only available source
Permission of The Courier-Journal

years ago we raised a lot of wheat and the soil produced fifty-two bushels of corn to the acre. It won't do it now....[40]

E.D. White estimated that the population of Wolf Island in 1942 was approximately 150. During that earlier period most of the land was in timber and farms were small, according to that local spokesman. Firms from Tennessee purchased the greater portion of the timberland on the island. Sizable stands of commercially-valuable trees included cottonwood, sycamore, and ash.[41] By 1954 Wolf Island's population had gradually declined to the extent that the isle was "inhabited by only about four permanent families," according to writer Jewell.[42]

At that time the timber companies had gained possession of about one-third of the land on the island. These operations continued their harvesting of the high-quality trees for pulpwood production. Important crops grown at that time included corn, cotton, and soybeans. Some farmers raised cattle, but the enterprise was handicapped by the limited number of fields on the island that were fenced.[43]

Columnist Craig reports that, according to White, "As farming became more mechanized, Missourians began to buy up the small farms on the island.... When the large-scale farmers and the timber companies moved in, most of the Wolf islanders moved off.... It was easier for the Missourians to get their farm trucks and equipment on and off the island."[44]

Even as later as 1954 travel on the island was normally restricted to "jeep, tractor and horseback."[45] The exception occurred during dry periods when cars could be driven on a dirt road extending through the center of the isle. No electricity was available yet, and water was still pumped from wells of the individual properties.[46]

In 1952 the Hickman County board of education had to close the remaining one-room school that had been serving the white children on Wolf Island "because of a total lack of students."[47] Since 1881 this school, or its preceding structures, had provided a regular term for the pupils of the isle. However, it was not unusual for classes to be cancelled "for a few days during high water."[48] Usually the teacher stayed on the island during the school week and went back to the mainland over the weekend. Teachers who taught in the Wolf Island school included Miss Montra Allen, Miss Carrie Baker, Mrs. W.A. Bunch, Mrs. Rubie Evans, and the Reverend B.E. Overbey.[49]

Writer Jewell provides a rather detailed description of the complexities involved in securing medical treatment when a Wolf Islander became ill:

> A doctor making a sick call to the island had to allow six hours for the round trip. Rupert Hickerson of Clinton, who a few years ago was a driver for the late Dr. J.F. Dunn of Arlington, tells of the rather involved procedure such a visit entailed. A neighbor of the sick man would drive his wagon to the chute where he would row to the Missouri mainland. He then walked to the ferry landing where he was taken to Columbus. There he called Dr. Dunn and waited at the ferry for him to arrive. Then they ferried back across the river, drove their automobile to the chute, rowed across the strait of water, and then went by wagon to the bedside of the sick. Then the process began in reverse. Six hours later Dr. Dunn was back in his office.[50]

The chute that then remained along the western side of the island spread out as it reached the main channel of the Mississippi to create a desolate beach -- one that was not littered with empty suntan oil containers but only with infrequent remnants of driftwood. This arresting expanse of sand was rarely disturbed by footprints and "to walk over it or any other part of Wolf Island [was] to be transported to another world."[51]

By 1963 water still stood in the chute, but when the level was low during dry weather residents forded the barrier with their automobiles. If inhabitants could get out at the appropriate time, they would still have to go upstream a short distance to the old site of Belmont to cross by ferry to Columbus in order to vote.[52] During that time the chute, usually dry at the upper end, was described as being anywhere from 100 to 150 feet[53] to as much as 100 yards[54] wide and from 20[55] to 25[56] feet deep. It was recalled that "much of the time people and farm equipment had to be ferried across it."[57] Property owners in 1962 constructed a bridge across the slough,[58] which would have given more dependability for passage. E.D. White, who purchased 400 acres of Wolf Island land in 1967 when the isle still had permanent occupants, recalled that in about 1972 "at his request" Hickman County build a gravel road which crossed the bridge at the head of Wolf Is-

LAST OF THE SCHOOLS - This is the last of Wolf Island school buildings. It was closed in 1952 because of a total lack of students. Educational facilities had been available since 1881 for the island's children. [1954]
Reprint from article photocopy as only available source
Permission of The Paducah Sun

land.[59] This landowner explained that the bridge was formed by "an old barge."[60]

Writer Powell in 1972 found that Wolf Island really was no longer an island nor even a community. He described in picturesque form the scene that confronted him:

> A large, well-kept white house, on a high foundation, gleams in the sun. Nearby are two sagging, decaying buildings that once were tenant houses. In the distance an old silo with vines creeping up the north side stands out against the sky.
>
> In the black, sandy soil of the area are pieces of broken dishes and rusted remnants of what once were household items. A boy's "agate" marble has been turned up by a plow.
>
> This is Wolf Island, once a community of perhaps 40 or 50 families and now the home of three people.[61]

Wolf Island by that time physically seemed to be a part of the state of Missouri since a long length of the slough that earlier kept the isle separate from its nearby state to the west had been filled with the accumulation of sand. The just-

48

WOLF ISLAND FERRY - The Columbus ferry on the Mississippi River is the pricipal means of communication between Wolf Island and the rest of the state of Kentucky. [1954]
Reprint from article photocopy as only available source
Permission of The Paducah Sun

completed gravel road gave further linkage between the earlier island and the now-joined mainland.[62]

The community that had existed on Wolf Island disappeared because a few people secured all the farmland that remained. By 1972 the cultivated area was being tilled as "one big soybean operation."[63]

However, this circumstance did not occur because of "a land-gobbling deal; it happened because of a scourge of nature known as Johnson grass."[64]

Earlier the farmers of small acreage had cultivated the fertile land in a setting familiar in other productive areas. Then the invader, the dreaded Johnson grass, commenced its relentless role as it began "to crowd and choke out the row crops."[65] The detested villain spread so quickly and was so overwhelming that nothing then could contend with it.[66]

In time the tillers of the small plots departed; large-scale farmers purchased the little farms and consolidated them into new large farms. Modern farming innovations soon introduced new machinery to the isle that allowed easier cul-

49

LONELY FOOTPRINTS - Few footprints are found on this quiet and lonely beach in Hickman County. The desolate area is on Wolf Island which is separated from the rest of Kentucky by the broad expanse of the Mississippi River but is only a stone's throw from Missouri. Slight dip in background indicates chute which separates the Kentucky island from Missouri. [1954]

Reprint from article photocopy as only available source
Permission of The Paducah Sun

tivation of the fields accompanied by the application of chemicals to suppress the Johnson grass that had been prevailing.[67]

Thus a single house "--stately in a broad expanse of land as loose and dark as an ask bank--" was all that remained of the earlier community located on Wolf Island. The occupants of the home, William and Bonnie Neal and their young son, rented the place from absentee owners who lived in Alabama. Neal worked in the vicinity operating heavy equipment for income.[68]

Mrs. Neal was quoted as saying, "It is lonely at night, but we like to be out here."[69]

The island, as it remained at least in name, was besieged during the conducive season each year by throngs of mosquitos, and rising waters edged near these residents' white house or even washed at the foundation about every second year.[70]

Wolf Island in 1972

Often the Neals were the only living souls in the large bottomland of this new adhesion to the Missouri mainland. Wolf Island, in its new form, included about 12,000 acres of fields and woodlands in 1972.[71]

During daylight hours the sole residents could see boats gliding by on the river, "their pilothouses riding high above the shoreline when the water [was] normal or high."[72]

Two brothers, Raymond and Murphy Morrow who lived in Bertrand, Missouri, owned and cultivated a portion of the acreage on the former isle. Possibly eight or ten other individuals owned the rest of the cultivatable land and the adjoining woodlands, the latter constituting approximately half of the entire realm.[73]

The unwelcome Johnson grass had already taken over their property when the Morrows arrived. Raymond Morrow recalled, "I remember driving a pickup truck through the grass and it was higher than the truck cab."[74]

The larger part of the tillable portion of Wolf Island, in its entirety then containing only about 12,000 acres after the eroding river had taken its toll, was devoted to the growing of the rising-market crop of soybeans. The rich bottomland that remained was still so fertile that fertilizer did not have to be applied, and an average yield of 40 bushels of soybeans an acre was secured.[75]

The Morrow brothers, as residents of Missouri who only commuted to Wolf Island to farm their land, had to purchase "non-resident licenses to fish from the island's riverbank and to hunt in its woods."[76] Before they discovered that these permits were required, the two had to pay a fine for a hunting violation on the isle.[77] Apparently fish and game wardens from the Kentucky mainland still made their way to Wolf Island at that time.

The then-recently built gravel road, about seven and a half miles in length and which cost the state of Kentucky approximately $20,000, traversed the filled-in slough at a point where the state line was marked only by "a line of trees."[78] Such was the official recognition of the states.

Mrs. John Watts, the former ferryboat-commuting schoolteacher for the isle, remembered "a post office and store which once served the island, but the settlement was Wolf Island, Mo., not Wolf Island, Ky."[79]

By 1979 Wolf Island was found by writer Craig to have been reduced in size to only 11,000 acres and to have been "uninhabited and owned mostly by residents of Tennessee and Missouri."(80) The distance across the Mississippi to the Kentucky mainland was estimated at about a mile. The former chute or slough to the west was then described as a "swampy, cottonwood-rimmed remains of what was the main river channel a century ago."(81)

At that time the Columbus-Belmont ferry still plied the Mississippi to maintain a link with the homeland,[82] even though no Kentucky residents remained on what was still called Wolf Island. Property owners, though now "alien," still had to pay county taxes to Hickman County and "file Kentucky income tax returns."[83]

Sometimes the ferry to and from Columbus did not operate because of mechanical breakdown or ice-jamming in the river. The next nearest ferry service was between Hickman, Kentucky and Dorena, Missouri, approximately 15 miles

Lonely landscape of Wolf Island [1979]

Staff Photo by Barry Craig
Reprint from article photocopy as only available source
Permission of The Paducah Sun

downstream from Columbus. The next closest crossing was about 25 miles upstream from Wolf Island by bridges over the Mississippi and Ohio rivers to enter Kentucky at Wickliffe.[84]

Clearly the times had changed for Wolf Island. Yet that visiting journalist in 1979 found reminders of days long past: "Evidences of habitation remain in weed-choked sites of a little wooden elementary school building and several houses. There is also an all-but-forgotten cemetery which contains headstones dating to the early 19th century."[85]

Endnotes

1. E. D. White, "Wolf Island Was Once Surrounded by Mississippi River" in *Jackson Purchase Historical Society Sesquicentennial Edition* (Mayfield, Kentucky: The Mayfield Messenger, 27 December 1969), p. 8.

2. Hall Allen, night editor, "The Wily Desperado," *The Paducah [Kentucky] Sun-Democrat*, 16 July 1954.

3. Allen.

4. *Ibid.*

5. *Ibid.*

6. *Ibid.*

7. Barry Craig, "Uninhabited Island Part of Kentucky," *The Paducah [Kentucky] Sun-Democrat*, 1 March 1979.

8. John S. Osborn, Jr., "Missouri vs Kentucky" in article sent to Mrs. N. D. Montgomery, Clinton, Kentucky attorney, 26 December 1963.

9. *State of Missouri vs State of Kentucky,* 11 Wall U.S. 395 (1870), *United States Supreme Court Reports, Lawyers Edition* (20 L Ed 116), (Rochester: Lawyers Co-operative Publishing Company, 1926), p. 119.

10. *Ibid.*

11. *Ibid.*, pp. 119-121.

12. Bill Powell, "Wolf Island is a Slice of Kentucky on the Missouri Side," *The Courier-Journal*, 30 May 1972.

13. White.

14. Harry Bosler, "Kentucky's Tight Little Island Is Slipping," *The Courier-Journal*, 5 January 1941.

15. *Ibid.*

16. White.

17. Craig.

18. *Ibid.*

19. White.

20. Virginia Jewell, "Stray Chunk of Kentucky," *The Paducah [Kentucky] Sun-Democrat*, 16 July 1954.

21. *Ibid.*

22. Bosler.

23. Jewell.

24. *Ibid.*

25. Powell.

26. *Ibid.*

27. *Ibid.*

28. Bosler.

29. *Ibid.*

30. *Ibid.*

31. *Ibid.*

32. *Ibid.*

33. *Ibid.*

34. *Ibid.*

35. *Ibid.*

36. *Ibid.*

37. *Ibid.*

38. *Ibid.*

39. *Ibid.*

40. *Ibid.*

41. Craig.

42. Jewell.

43. *Ibid.*

44. Craig.

45. Jewell.

46. *Ibid.*

47. *Ibid.*

48. *Ibid.*

49. *Ibid.*

50. *Ibid.*

51. *Ibid.*

52. Osborn.

53. White.

54. Powell.
55. *Ibid.*
56. White.
57. Powell.
58. *Ibid.*
59. *Ibid.*
60. *Ibid.*
61. *Ibid.*
62. *Ibid.*
63. *Ibid.*
64. *Ibid.*
65. *Ibid.*
66. *Ibid.*
67. Ibid.
68. *Ibid.*
69. *Ibid.*
70. *Ibid.*
71. *Ibid.*
72. *Ibid.*
73. *Ibid.*
74. *Ibid.*
75. *Ibid.*
76. *Ibid.*
77. *Ibid.*
78. *Ibid.*
79. *Ibid.*
80. Craig.
81. *Ibid.*
82. *Ibid.*
83. *Ibid.*
84. *Ibid.*
85. *Ibid.*

3

KENTUCKY BEND, KENTUCKY

Kentucky Bend: A Little Chip Off The Big Block

Kentucky Bend

3A

Kentucky Bend: A Struggle For Political Identity

Nowhere else in the United States is there to be found anything comparable to Kentucky Bend. Located in the extreme southwestern part of Kentucky, this portion of Fulton County is completely isolated from the rest of the state. In fact, it is surrounded by the Mississippi River and the state of Missouri on three sides and is bounded on the remaining side by the state of Tennessee. (Fig. 1)

Residents of Kentucky Bend must travel more than thirty-five miles by highway and pass through Tennessee to get to the county seat, Hickman, located further upstream on the "mainland." In the event the inhabitants of this outpost do not wish to enter Tennessee, a second land route would involve crossing the Mississippi River on their own and securing land transportation across a portion of Missouri over poor roads to a town where ferry service might be used to cross the Mississippi once again to reach Hickman.[1] The last alternative would be a meandering boat trip upstream and even this river route presumably would pass through portions of the channel belonging to one or the other, or both, of these interposing states. Only the first alternative is practical.

These marooned Kentuckians live in an area known locally by at least three names: Kentucky Bend, Madrid Bend, and New Madrid Bend. Madrid Bend actually is used to identify a larger area which extends southward into Lake County, Tennessee between Reelfoot Lake on the east and the Mississippi River on the west.[2] However, many inhabitants of the area reserve this designation for the portion located in Kentucky. Others refer (more appropriately) to this lobe as Kentucky Bend.[3] New Madrid Bend is a more direct reference to the old town of New Madrid, Missouri, situated along the northernmost part of the bend in the river and furnishing the name for both this limited area in Kentucky as well as the more general region just described. Obviously there is some confusion and much overlapping in names. This was discovered in conversation[4] as well as in the use of maps and written material during research efforts. For the purpose of this study, the term Kentucky Bend, or simply the Bend, will be used wherever possible.

The dimensions of Kentucky Bend have been determined largely by the meandering of the Mississippi River. According to investigation by the Mississippi River Commission, nearly the entire area of present-day Kentucky Bend lies upon former beds of both the Mississippi and Ohio rivers. (Fig. 2) More recent changes in location and size are shown in Figures 3 and 4. Jewell states that "geologists are amazed that at this point of America's geography it is the sharpest bend in the Mississippi River, and what is more, is the only point where Missouri is on the east side and the river flows northward."[5] It may be noted that a similar situation exists just upstream from Cairo, Illinois. The boundaries

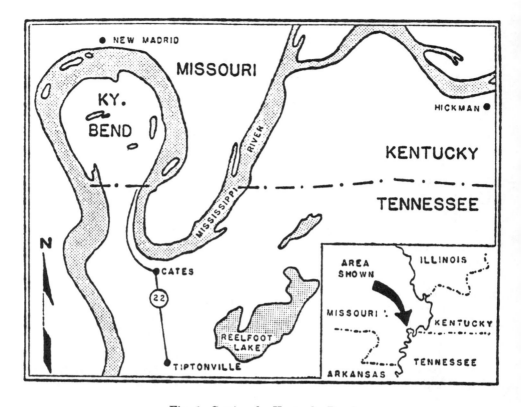

Fig. 1 - Setting for Kentucky Bend
Adapted from map by Lee Ebner. Source: Al Allen, "An Old Kentucky Home Where The Sun Shines Last," *The Courier-Journal & Times Magazine*, pp. 17-20, March 14, 1976.

of Kentucky Bend certainly present one of the more curious features of this area. To the casual map observer the present boundaries alone may appear as a strange enough phenomenon, but the account of their establishment is perhaps equally remarkable.

The earliest boundary affecting this area dates from a line established by the Treaty of Paris (1763) which stated:

> In order to re-establish peace and solid and durable foundations, and to remove for ever all subjects of dispute with regard to the limits of the British and French territories on the continent of America, that for the future, the confines between the dominions of his Britannic majesty in that part of the world, shall be fixed irrevocably by a line drawn along the middle of the river Mississippi, from its source to the river Iberville;. . . [6]

Thus the treaty appeared to set "irrevocably" a boundary line that would later serve briefly as the western border of the United States and eventually become a state boundary line for part of Kentucky Bend.

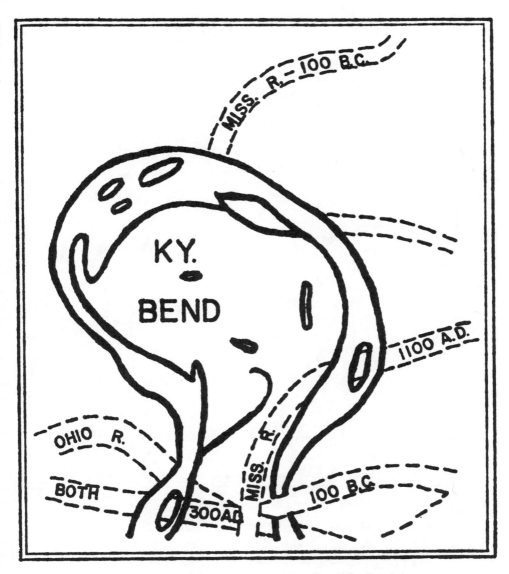

Fig. 2 - Ancient River Courses Of The Kentucky Bend Area
Adapted from Plate 22, Sheet 2, Geological Investigation, Mississippi River Alluvial Valley, 1944. Ancient courses of the Mississippi River Meander Belt.

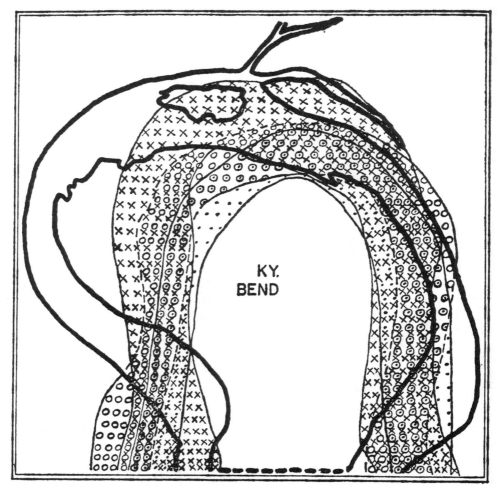

Fig. 3 - Early Channel Shifts Affecting Kentucky Bend

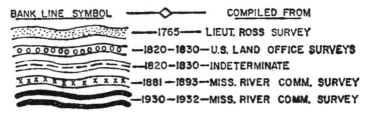

BANK LINE SYMBOL ——————◇—————— COMPILED FROM
————1765——— LIEUT. ROSS SURVEY
—1820–1830—U.S. LAND OFFICE SURVEYS
—1820–1830—INDETERMINATE
—1881—1893—MISS. RIVER COMM. SURVEY
—1930—1932—MISS. RIVER COMM. SURVEY

ADAPTED FROM LOWER MISSISSIPPI RIVER EARLY STREAM CHANNELS AT APPROXIMATE HALF-CENTURY INTERVALS, CAIRO, ILL.. TO BATON ROUGE, LA., MILE 0 TO MILE 842, PREPARED IN THE OFFICE OF THE PRESIDENT, MISSISSIPPI RIVER COMMISSION, VICKSBURG, MISS., AUG. 1938.

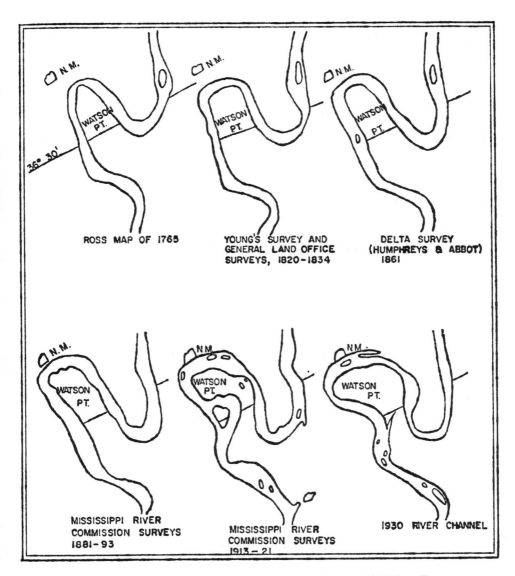

Fig. 4 - The Dimensions of Kentucky Bend During Different Eras
Source: Progressive channel changes, lower Mississippi River, 1765 to 1930, Plate VI
(2) - Cairo to Bend of Island No. 40. D. O. Elliot. Mississippi River Flood Control and
Navigation, 1932.

After Kentucky and Missouri had entered the union the two states became involved in a lengthy dispute over the ownership of Wolf Island located further upstream. In *Missouri v. Kentucky* (9 Wall, 395) the Supreme Court in 1870 awarded the island to Kentucky by ruling that "the boundary between Kentucky and Missouri is the middle of the Mississippi River, as stipulated in the treaty between Great Britain, France and Spain in 1763." The Court stated that "the line is the channel as it was then, and subsequent changes in the channel are of no effect." The decision was based on the finding that Wolf Island appeared "to have been east of the middle of the channel both in 1763, the date of the treaty, and 1820, the date when Missouri was admitted to the union and its boundary fixed by the same line."

The boundary description in 1944 for Kentucky Bend asserts that "the boundary with Missouri runs down the middle of the Mississippi River...from a point where the Kentucky-Tennessee line intersects the middle of the Mississippi for the second time, between New Madrid, Missouri, and Island No. 10, down the middle of the Mississippi to a point where the line intersects for the third time, near Compromise, Kentucky".[7] Though the wording for the boundary description is "runs" in the present tense with no time basis stated for the location of the middle of the river, it is noteworthy that the description includes reference to Compromise, Kentucky, established about 1819 or 1820. This little settlement on the western side of the Bend "was totally destroyed by encroachment of the Mississippi river" by about 1881, according to a local historian in the area.[8] Thus it appears the "middle-of-the-river" boundary describes a line appropriate to the early or middle nineteenth century, perhaps based on the Supreme Court ruling in *Missouri v. Kentucky* in 1870. If so, this would continue in effect that original "irrevocable" line and it still would be applicable regardless of the river's present location.

Hardin appears to support this position in repeating the wording of the *Missouri v. Kentucky* decision as he contends that "the line is the channel as it was then, and subsequent changes in the channel have been declared of no effect."[9] Current maps reveal that a number of states which have the Mississippi River as a common boundary have brief segments departing from the present river course usually representing previous channel locations.

A glance at the location of the Mississippi River in 1765 (Fig. 3) will give some idea of the approximate position of the bed of the river at that time; from this may be reconstructed the approximate boundary line which was then decreed and which by law is still in effect if indeed it is "irrevocable." On this basis it would seem a question could be raised regarding the present ownership of the northwest portion of the Bend. On the other hand, this contention may be in error and there may exist the concept of a "practical" boundary line between the two states that continues to be marked as the middle of the shifting channel of the Mississippi. Detailed maps of Kentucky Bend often show such a midstream boundary that could not coincide with the one of 1763.

The boundary between Kentucky Bend and Tennessee eventually was decided by compromise after a long period of uncertainty, dissatisfaction, and controversy. At least one familiar map shows that before settlement of the Bend no state boundary was designated in this area. Commenting on Elihu Barker's map of 1794, Jillson analyzes the situation:

> In western Kentucky one notes, with interest, the omission of a separating line between Kentucky and Tennessee west of the Cumberland River. The grievous errors of the early boundary surveys run by Dr. Thomas Walker and others westwardly along the 36 30' from Cumberland Gap had already made itself felt throughout the western country. As argument matched argument, dissensions rose to the point that no cartographer dared draw the line . . . (Barker) met this highly controversial situation by a complete admission of ignorance. Southwestern Kentucky . . . was in 1794 - according to the best authorities and surveys - a blank.[10]

This was the situation two years after Kentucky had gained statehood!

The earliest attempt to locate a dividing line was apparently made in 1779 when the legislatures of North Carolina and Virginia, responding to the pressing demands of western settlers, appointed a joint commission for the purpose of extending their common boundary. As the line was run westward, a disagreement occurred between North Carolina surveyors Colonel Richard Henderson and William B. Smith and Virginia surveyors Thomas Walker and Daniel Smith. The two commissions separated and ran parallel lines at a distance of about two miles apart. Henderson's line run by the Carolina commission was continued only as far as Cumberland Mountain. There Henderson and Smith stopped after protesting by letter Walker's line being run to the south of theirs. The Virginia commissioners continued their line westward, but due to their failure to make correct allowance for the variation of the needle the line "deflected continuously to the north." When they reached the Tennessee River the surveyors were at approximately thirty-six degrees and forty minutes, about seventeen miles too far downstream. "Though not authorized to extend the line" beyond this point, Walker and Smith "proceeded to mark its termination on the Mississippi, but did not survey the intervening distance." The Henderson line, if it had been extended west from Cumberland Mountain with the same needle variance, would have been even further north of the intended line of thirty-six degrees and thirty minutes as it reached the Mississippi River.[11]

The legislatures of the states took no immediate action over the disagreement of their commissioners. Later in 1789 and 1790, the legislature of North Carolina concurred with two reports made by the Committee on Boundaries, chaired by General Thomas Person, which led to a law establishing Walker's Line as the boundary with Virginia. Garrett contends that "the action thus adopting Walker's Line as clearly extended it to the Mississippi as if posts had been placed every five miles between." In 1791, the legislature of Virginia confirmed this line. "Thus the boundary line was regarded by both states as finally settled."[12]

But in 1792 Tennessee, during the term of office of Territorial Governor William Blount, repudiated the North Carolina and Virginia compact. This led Kentucky to reopen the boundary question. This interest on the part of officials in Kentucky was prompted no doubt by their discovery that Walker's Line was several miles north of the previously designated parallel of thirty-six degrees and thirty minutes, where Kentucky now insisted the boundary should be located.[13]

An act was passed in 1813 by Kentucky which contained the suggestion of impatience over the continuation of the strife and insisted upon discovering a satisfactory solution: "Whereas it appears . . . that the legislature of the state of Tennessee . . . have indicated a disposition to depart from the proposition formerly made by their government to this, of proceeding . . . to ascertain by correct and scientific observation, the true line of separation between the respective states, . . . the disagreeable necessity [is] imposed upon the government of Kentucky . . . of having that long contested question finally settled by a resort to the means pointed out by the constitution of the United States . . ."[14] Tennessee retaliated with an act in 1815 which decreed Walker's Line to be the official boundary between the states:

> Whereas, some difficulty has existed between the State of Kentucky and this State respecting the boundary between them, and whereas it is essential to the harmony and interest of both states, that the line commonly called Walker's line, heretofore considered, and acted on, as the boundary between them, should be established as the boundary between the two states, therefore:
>
> Sec. 1. Be it enacted [italics in the original] . . . That the line commonly called Walker's line be, and the name is hereby established and confirmed as the true boundary between the States of Kentucky and this state.
>
> Sec. 5. Be it enacted [italics in the original], That if the Legislature of Kentucky shall refuse to pass such an act as the above stated, then this act shall cease to be in force . . .[15]

The next year Kentucky responded with an act which insisted upon the designation of the parallel of thirty-six degrees and thirty minutes latitude as the state boundary west of the Tennessee River:

> . . . at the west extremity of Walker's line, to wit, at the Tennessee River, a line shall be extended up or down said river (as the case may require) till it reaches the true chartered latitude thirty-six degrees and thirty minutes north; and from that point the line shall be extended due west, still keeping the same latitude, till it reaches the river Mississippi.[16]

The state of Tennessee in 1817 did not agree to this demand, and held to the Walker line:

> Sec. 3. . . . That this state will, provided the State of Kentucky agree thereto, apply to the executive of the United States, to appoint a commissioner to ascertain the true point, where the boundary line between this state and the state of Kentucky, will strike the Tennessee river on the western bank thereof, and that from that point, a line shall be run directly west to the western boundary of the state of Tennessee, which shall be the line between the two states.[17]

If the states had agreed to act upon Tennessee's proposal to have a commissioner appointed to determine the true point at which the Walker line reached the Tennessee River for the purpose of extending the line directly west to the

Mississippi River to complete the boundary, it would appear likely that the line actually surveyed by Walker would have been located from the original tree chops. This line, farther north than the point at which Walker first reached the Tennessee River as first projected and earlier described, was referred to by Sames as "Walker's upper line" and "is not mentioned in Smith's report in 1779-80."[18]

Had Tennessee gained its wish, there would have been no Kentucky Bend. Its line of insistence would not have touched at any point the loop of the Mississippi River forming the Bend that eventually was to be awarded to the state of Kentucky. This line would have intersected the Mississippi River perhaps forty-five miles upstream to the northeast of the termination of the final boundary line. The entire area within the meander then unquestionably would have belonged to Tennessee. (Fig. 5)

Kentucky undertook the next decisive step in 1818 by passing a "spicy enactment" which specified a boundary for the Bend to be run on the line representing the measurement of thirty-six degrees and thirty minutes north latitude:

> Be it enacted [italics in the original] . . . That all laws heretofore passed by the general assembly of this commonwealth relative to the boundary line between this state and the state of Tennessee, shall be, and the same are hereby repealed.
> Sec. 2. . . . That the southern boundary line of this state shall be and remain on a line running west from the top of Cumberland mountain to the Mississippi river in thirty-six degrees and thirty minutes north latitude, anything in any former law passed by this state to the contrary notwithstanding.[19]

This was followed in 1819 by the dispatch of two surveyors, Robert Alexander and Luke Munsell, to run and mark the line upon this parallel, specified in the new act, between the Tennessee and Mississippi rivers. Upon completion, this was then declared "to be the true boundary."[20] This line, however, actually ran south of the specified parallel by about four hundred feet.[21] The error apparently resulted from triangulation from an incorrectly calculated point on the Mississippi River where the boundary would first strike, just west of Reelfoot Lake.

Tennessee felt compelled to compromise in order to retain land in question east of the Tennessee River. Thus in 1820 the boundary problem was tackled by commissioners from the two states. The result was that Walker's Line was agreed upon as far west as the Tennessee River where the line was to run upstream to the termination of Alexander and Munsell's Line which was recognized as the boundary line from this point westward to the Mississippi River.[22] In 1821, a line was run by W.T. Henderson, the survey superintendent for Kentucky's Jackson Purchase area, which followed precisely Alexander and Munsell's Line across Kentucky Bend.[23] All was then quiet on the southern boundary of the Bend until 1845 when Tennessee commissioners Clement W. Nance and William P. McLain met Kentucky commissioners Sandford Duncan and Constant A. Wilson for the purpose of carrying out instructions of their respective states to run and mark the boundary once again in this area which

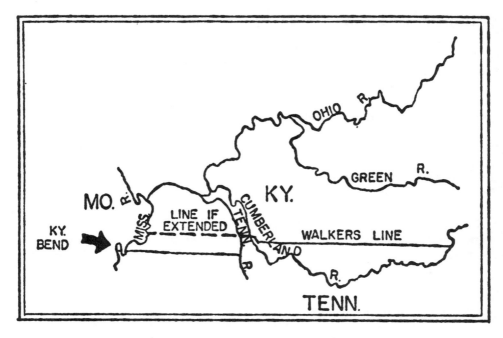

Fig. 5 - Effect Of The Proposed Extension of Walker's Line On Kentucky Bend
Adapted from map accompanying article by Bayless E. Hardin, "The Kentucky Boundary," The Register Of The Kentucky State Historical Society, 44 (January, 1946), 1-32.

included Kentucky Bend. Here they followed the Alexander and Munsell line of 1819.[24]

In 1859 the states appointed a joint commission to designate the permanent boundary in the area. The commissioners reported that they "met at a place called Compromise, a small settlement on the Mississippi River, and having improved instruments made an accurate and satisfactory survey."[25] They started this final line just south of Compromise, located in latitude thirty-six degrees, twenty-nine minutes, and fifty-six seconds, which they noted was too far south by about four hundred feet. The line (Fig. 6) was run eastward from this point following the one marked by earlier commissioners with certain local exceptions mentioned in the report.[26]

The line was marked on trees with four chops facing toward both the east and the west.[27] A distance of five feet was also cleared on each side of the line and trees facing the boundary line were marked with "K" and "T", the initials of the two states.[28]

Stone posts were set up along the entire boundary at regular intervals. The commissioners reported that these posts cost more than had been anticipated. Because "there were no stones west of the Tennessee River," according to these

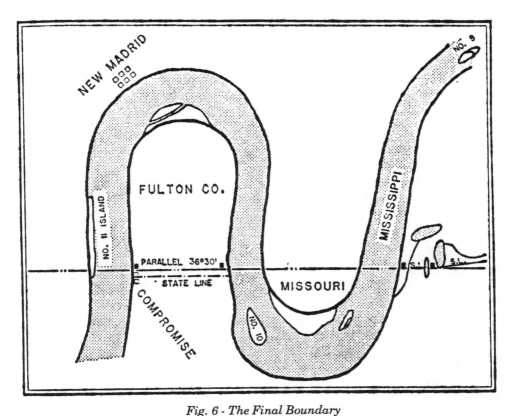

Fig. 6 - The Final Boundary
Source: The Report of the Boundary Line Commissioners of Kentucky and Tennessee
to the Honorable Isham G. Harris, Governor of Tennessee - November 11, 1859.

officials, they had to be imported. Part of a shipment of stones was brought by
boat and unloaded at Compromise. Although stone posts were to be erected at
distances of five miles, the first marker west of Compromise was placed at a distance of ten miles on the Kentucky "mainland," since a five mile post would have
fallen across the river in the intervening bend belonging to Missouri.[29] In the
report the commissioners refer to the Camp Watson Observatory, and in a
remark column they record the information that Camp Watson is seventy-seven
hundred and sixty-three feet north of the first "station" east of Compromise.[30]

The establishment of the boundary was made official when the acts of the commissioners were confirmed by both Kentucky and Tennessee in 1860.[31] With
this last boundary line now delineating the southern border of Kentucky Bend,
attention may be turned directly to the Bend itself. The significant fact, as far
as this story is concerned, is that Kentucky claimed, acquired, and has retained
this isolated lobe. At the beginning of the last survey just described, "the commissioners were confronted with a problem which constitutes one of the most

Chops and "K" Letters on Boundary Trees

unusual features included within the boundary of Kentucky . . . The Tennessee commissioners claimed that New Madrid Bend, being cut off from Kentucky by the intervening reverse curve of the river which interposed a portion of Missouri, should naturally be included as a part of Tennessee." The commissioners from Kentucky maintained that the agreement stipulated that all of the territory north of thirty-six degrees and thirty minutes and lying between the Mississippi and Tennessee rivers was to belong to Kentucky. Kentucky Bend met this requirement. Since Tennessee had gained advantages east of this area during the boundary settlement, "the Kentucky commissioners demanded a strict construction. Accordingly, the small neighborhood, including only a few square miles and a few hundred people, was attached to Kentucky, and became a part of Fulton County."[32]

Several attempts have been made by Tennessee to acquire this tract of land.[33] In an effort to relieve the inhabitants of the Bend from the peculiar hardships of such a condition, Tennessee governor James D. Porter in 1877 appointed two commissions to negotiate with Kentucky for this area, but "Kentucky was inexorable, and nothing was accomplished."[34] A more recent effort to have Kentucky Bend annexed by the state of Tennessee reportedly had the support or at least the approval of both United States district congressmen and the secretaries of state of the two states. Supposedly even Fulton County, the "mother county," was agreeable to annexation.[35] Officials of that county must not have believed their local sentiments were being accurately expressed. At any rate, the transfer did not take place.

A strong expression of state loyalty and opposition to any move to have the area added to Tennessee has always come from the generally-acknowledged patriarch of Kentucky Bend, "the community's unofficial leader and elder statesman," eighty-five-year-old [at that time] Alfred Stepp, who has the largest farm on the Bend.[36] Stepp, who first leased acreage on Kentucky Bend in 1927 while still residing in his native New Madrid County, Missouri, moved across the river permanently in 1938, acquired title to his land, and began the development of his model farm.[37] This leading citizen acknowledges some personal and political opposition, both on and off the Bend, while still maintaining the respect and friendship of many citizens of the area. He did mention that one Tennessean owning land in the Bend (who would remain unidentified) favored annexation by his state based on the contention that such a shift would result in better roads and education. But Stepp claimed the real reason for this absentee owner's sentiments was the larger cotton base he would be granted for his acreage if it were in Tennessee.

Mr. Stepp fears the higher taxes that would be assessed if the Bend should become a part of Tennessee. During the last threat to Kentucky's outpost, he put through a call to the governor of the state expressing his concern about the future status of the Bend. The governor told him not to worry or lose any sleep. So Stepp believes he will not have to move to remain a Kentuckian as long as he lives.[38] A Tiptonville, Tennessee official, who owns land on the Bend, agrees. He points out that existing property taxes in Kentucky and Tennessee do not differ greatly for comparable land. This spokesman, who has strong family ties to the earlier history of Kentucky Bend, concludes that no move to have this isolated area annexed by Tennessee will be successful as long as Stepp is alive.[39]

Thus - for the forseeable future - Kentucky Bend appears to remain safe as a dot making its contribution to a reclining exclamation point depicting the outline of the state.

Endnotes

1. Onida Jewell, "A River Finds a Mystery - and Madrid Bend is Born," *The Fulton* [Kentucky] *News*, October 12, 1951.

2. *Ibid.*

3. R.C. Donaldson, "Pioneer Life In Madrid Bend, Kentucky," *Lake County* [Tennessee] *Banner*, July 25, 1947.

4. One resident referred to his locality as "Madrid Bend" while sitting in a truck, the door of which was lettered with the name of the farm owner followed by the words "Kentucky Bend."

5. Jewell, "River."

6. Robert K. Cullen and L.C. Turner (ed.), *Notes and Annotations to the Kentucky Revised Statutes* (The Kentucky Revision Commission, 1944), p. 4.

7. *Ibid.*

8. Emmett Lewis, "Town of Compromise Swept into the River," *Lake County* [Tennessee] *Banner*, February 6, 1975.

9. Bayless E. Hardin, "The Kentucky Boundary," *The Register of the Kentucky Historical Society*, 44 (January, 1946), 29.

10. Willard Rouse Jillson, *Pioneer Kentucky* (Frankfort: The State Journal Company, 1934), p. 35.

11. W.R. Garrett, *History of the South Carolina Cession and the Northern Boundary of Tennessee* (Nashville: Southern Methodist Publishing House, 1884), pp. 12-20.

12. *Ibid.*

13. *History of Tennessee* (Nashville: The Goodspeed Publishing Company, 1887), p. 176.

14. *Littell's Laws of Kentucky* (5 vols.; Frankfort: William Hunter, 1809-1819), IV, 388-89.

15. *Acts Passed at the First Session of the Eleventh General Assembly of the State of Tennessee* (Nashville: T.G. Bradford, 1815), pp. 241-42.

16. *Littell's Laws of Kentucky*, V, 401-402.

17. *Acts Passed at the First Session of the Twelfth General Assembly of the State of Tennessee* (Knoxville: George Wilson, 1817), pp. 191-92.

18. James W. Sames, III, *Four Steps West* (Versailles: James W. Sames, III, 1971), p. 96.

19. *Acts Passed at the First Session of the Twenty-Seventh General Assembly for the Commonwealth of Kentucky* (Frankfort: Kendall and Russells, 1819), pp. 437-38.

20. Garrett, *History*, p. 24.

21. Sames, *Four Steps West*, p. 109.

22. *History of Tennessee*, p. 179.

23. *Report of the Boundary Line Commissioners of Kentucky and Tennessee, to the Honorable Isham G. Harris, Governor of Tennessee*, November 11, 1859, p. 3. State Historical Library, Nashville, Tennessee.

24. Hardin, "The Kentucky Boundary," pp. 16-17.

25. *History of Tennessee*, p. 179.

26. *Report of the Boundary Line Commissioners*, p. 3.

27. *History of Tennessee*, p. 180.

28. Garrett, *History*, p. 29.

29. *Report of the Boundary Line Commissioners*, pp. 3-4.

30. *Ibid.*, p. 5.

31. Garrett, *History*, p. 30.

32. Hardin, "The Kentucky Boundary," p. 18.

33. *Ibid.*

34. W.R. Garrett, "Northern Boundary of Tennessee," *The American Historical Magazine*, VI (1901), 37.

35. Interview with Winston Tipton, Tiptonville, Tennessee businessman, March 24, 1977.

36. B. Drummond Ayres, Jr., "Isolation Irks a Cut-Off Slice of Kentucky," *The New York Times*, March 8, 1972; also carried in *The Fulton County* [Kentucky] *News*, May 11, 1972.

37. *Ibid.*

38. Interview with Alfred Stepp, March 22, 1977.

39. Interview with Judge Wilford Parks, Jr., County Judge, Lake County, Tennessee, March 22, 1977.

"Steamboat 'Round Kentucky Bend - A Golden Era", by Allen Anthony, is reprinted from *The Register Of The Kentucky Historical Society,* ©1979, Volume 77, No. 1 (Winter 1979), pp. 25-29, by permission of The Kentucky Historical Society.

3B

Steamboat 'Round Kentucky Bend - A Golden Era

The area known today as Kentucky Bend, among other designations, has always had an unusual if not unique setting. Since official boundaries were finally determined, this unattached portion of Fulton County in the extreme southwestern part of the state of Kentucky has remained isolated within a loop of the Mississippi River, surrounded on three sides by the state of Missouri and on the remaining border by the state of Tennessee. (Figs. 1 and 2)

The settlement by English families of what later became known as Kentucky Bend appears to have begun shortly after the two significant events of 1811 occurred - the Great Earthquake of 1811-12, centered near the early Missouri town of New Madrid located across the river, and the almost simultaneous arrival of the first steamboat to appear on the Mississippi. The number of residents on the Bend itself remained small in the early decades. But from the beginning life was by nature and necessity closely tied to the river, which largely defined and served this remote area, even though the neck of the greater bend provided an outlet through Tennessee.

Transportation improved as these early years passed. The steamboat traffic was increasing, and a landing was established on the west bank of Kentucky Bend (Fig. 2), presumably at the home of Daniel Watson, which would mark the beginning of Watson's Landing, the first of many such small landings to be formed in later years. Also the cow path or Indian trail, running northward from the tentative state line toward the point opposite New Madrid, was improved until a road extended the length of the Bend, connecting with ferry service[1] northward across to New Madrid, and continuing southward below the state line to Obionville and points beyond. By 1839, Burr's map (Fig. 4) shows post offices at New Madrid and Obionville were connected by ferry and a "1 horse mail Post Coach Road or Sulkey." It is interesting to note that while Bartholomew's map (Fig. 5) and Johnson's earlier map (Fig. 6) show a post road but no ferry connection, Johnson's later map (Fig. 7) designates the ferry service - but no existing post road. Burr's map goes a step further by showing the post road spanning the width of the river - without ferry service. Watson's map (Fig. 8) of a later date hardly does justice to the size and shape of the Bend, not to mention the omission of the state boundary line with Tennessee. Bradford's map (Fig. 3) leaves doubt as to its accuracy in general. During the railroad building era, consideration reportedly was given to the feasibility of building a railroad line through the Bend with New Madrid as the northern terminus.[2] This proposal failed to materialize.

As settlement on the Bend advanced, the need arose for church and school to supplement that which could be offered in the home. A local authority explained

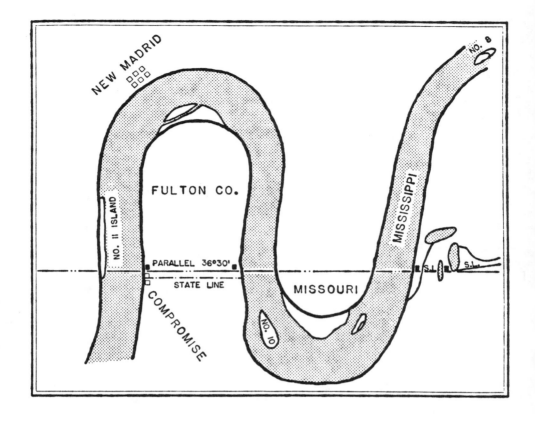

Fig. 1
SOURCE: THE REPORT OF THE BOUNDARY LINE COMMISSIONERS OF KEN-
TUCKY AND TENNESSEE TO THE HONORABLE ISHAM G. HARRIS, GOVER-
NOR OF TENNESSEE - NOVEMBER 11, 1859

that both of these institutions probably held meetings or classes in homes at first, until structures could be built. The first church, he ventures a guess, was built about 1832, or at least soon thereafter. The school was established probably by 1852.[3] Definite dates of origin were not found.

According to the writing of Mark Twain, this first church, or at least a church, was located at Compromise, the western terminus of the state boundary, (Fig. 1). He gives a colorful description of its setting and members, as well as revealing a tale of a continuing feud between the Watsons and the Darnells of Tennessee, neighbors on each side of the state line as well as fellow church members.[4] The story supposedly was related to Twain by a native of this region while the two were passengers on a steamboat passing around the Bend.

The economy of the Bend from the beginning was based heavily upon farming. For about the first seventy years, corn and wheat were the dominant crops,[5] al-

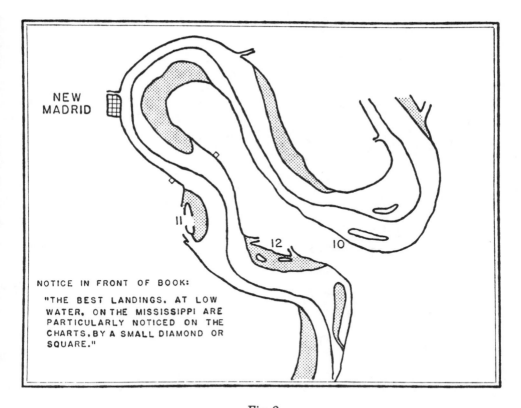

NEW
MADRID

NOTICE IN FRONT OF BOOK:

"THE BEST LANDINGS, AT LOW
WATER, ON THE MISSISSIPPI ARE
PARTICULARLY NOTICED ON THE
CHARTS, BY A SMALL DIAMOND OR
SQUARE."

Fig. 2
SOURCE: MISS. NO. 6 (1819, 20, 21 AND LATER SURVEYS) SAMUEL CUMING,
THE WESTERN PILOT, 1829.

though cotton early gained a foothold and was pushing steadily to the front.
Slavery was an important factor until ended by the Civil War. Thereafter, ad-
justment had to be made which brought in the familiar tenant and sharecrop-
per system. It was natural that in the area some fishing was done. With the
increased travel of steamboats up and down the river, there quickly developed
a market for firewood readily cut from the wooded portions of the Bend. When
owned and operated from the Kentucky side, ferry service provided limited
revenue for the enterpriser involved.

The population of Kentucky Bend was rapidly increasing. From a total of 2 in
1820, the number of inhabitants had risen to 303 by census count in 1870, to
332 in 1880,[6] and then dropped only slightly to 322 in 1890.[7] Many names appeared as landowners by this time (Fig. 9). Smaller farms were developing. Almost all the land was now in cultivation, with only one field of grass indicated.
The northern tip remained in woodland, but even this area was giving way to
cleared spaces.

77

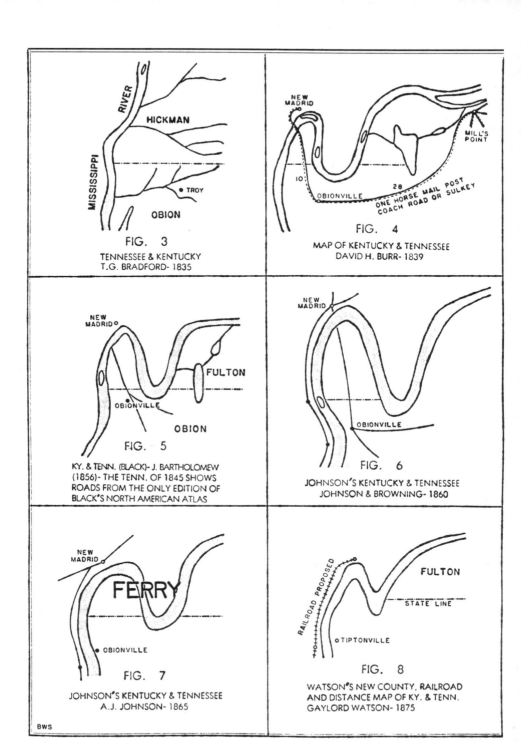

FIG. 3
TENNESSEE & KENTUCKY
T.G. BRADFORD- 1835

FIG. 4
MAP OF KENTUCKY & TENNESSEE
DAVID H. BURR- 1839

FIG. 5
KY. & TENN. (BLACK)- J. BARTHOLOMEW
(1856)- THE TENN. OF 1845 SHOWS
ROADS FROM THE ONLY EDITION OF
BLACK'S NORTH AMERICAN ATLAS

FIG. 6
JOHNSON'S KENTUCKY & TENNESSEE
JOHNSON & BROWNING- 1860

FIG. 7
JOHNSON'S KENTUCKY & TENNESSEE
A.J. JOHNSON- 1865

FIG. 8
WATSON'S NEW COUNTY, RAILROAD
AND DISTANCE MAP OF KY. & TENN.
GAYLORD WATSON- 1875

BWS

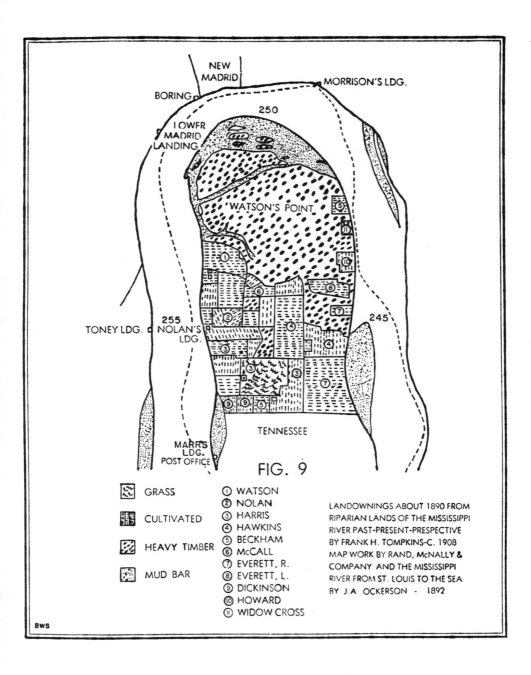

FIG. 9

GRASS   ① WATSON

CULTIVATED   ② NOLAN
   ③ HARRIS
   ④ HAWKINS

HEAVY TIMBER   ⑤ BECKHAM
   ⑥ McCALL

MUD BAR   ⑦ EVERETT, R.
   ⑧ EVERETT, L.
   ⑨ DICKINSON
   ⑩ HOWARD
   ⑪ WIDOW CROSS

LANDOWNINGS ABOUT 1890 FROM
RIPARIAN LANDS OF THE MISSISSIPPI
RIVER PAST-PRESENT-PRESPECTIVE
BY FRANK H. TOMPKINS-C. 1908
MAP WORK BY RAND, McNALLY &
COMPANY AND THE MISSISSIPPI
RIVER FROM ST. LOUIS TO THE SEA
BY J.A OCKERSON - 1892

BWS

79

"Steamboat trade was booming everywhere in the fifties...,"[8] and Kentucky Bend maintained a steady dependence upon this service for at least a half century until well after 1900. Landings were established wherever trade would warrant. Hunter states that "virtually every plantation touching the riverbank . . .had its own landing."[9] This, essentially, was the situation on the Bend. These landings appeared and disappeared by name with changes in farm ownership and channel movement. Watson's landing was soon followed by Harris's Landing and then later came Compromise (Fig.1), Noland's Landing (Fig. 9), and Kentucky Point.[10] In 1890 eight different landings were recognized officially for this year on both sides of the river in its meander around the Bend, with three being located on the Kentucky side.[11] In other years, Carrigan's Flat, Adam's Landing, another Harris's Landing,[12] Moss Landing, and another State Line Landing appeared for various durations on the western side of the Bend. Another landing was remembered on the eastern side around 1900, but its name was not recalled.[13]

One need for increased shipping service was the rapid success of cotton growing in Kentucky Bend. Corn and wheat gave way to this new money crop which had come into real prominence by the turn of the century. One former resident recalled that in 1900 practically all the fields were planted in cotton.[14]

Kentucky Bend was once "a rich prosperous area," recalled an old-timer who moved into the area in 1894 when he was eighteen years old. School one year opened with 110 pupils enrolled. New Madrid was well utilized as a trading and banking center.[15] Steamboats brought money and mail from St. Louis and Memphis.[16] The mail was carried during these years from the ferry and steamboat landing at Kentucky Point by road to Bessie, Tennessee, just south of the state line, for further distribution. Steamboats stopped at the various landings to leave such necessities as meat and other groceries, and cotton, the latter first in "snakes" and then later in bales. Of course, passengers were accepted and discharged upon request.[17] One could even disembark at a landing near the state line in the late evening, get a good night's sleep in a home, cross the narrow neck of the bend the next morning, and reboard the same steamer to continue his trip up or down the river.[18]

Arrangements were very informal and schedules often uncertain, but sometimes unusual consideration was shown and service given. An old former resident vividly remembers one day hailing a steamboat heading upstream in the channel not far off shore. The captain yelled out, "What do you want?" The farmer shouted back, "Need two tons of hay for my cattle!" The captain waved and continued on around the bend. About a week or so later on his way back downstream he pulled into the farmer's landing - to unload the two tons of hay.[19]

The economy retained its emphasis on agriculture with the shift to cotton. A small gin was in operation for a period on the Bend. One or two sawmills were begun[20] as timber was cut from the remaining wooded areas. An outside lumber and wood products company at one time owned over two sections known as the Mengel Estate and located in the northern portion of the Bend. Fishing and ferry boat service continued as smaller sources of income for those involved.

Photo by Don Cravens
Steamboat passengers used to get off, re-board the boat on the other side
Reprint from article photocopy as only available source
Permission of The Nashville Tennesseean

Later in this period the J.F. Adams store did business on the Bend and was located just south of the schoolhouse receiving some of its goods from boats, but securing most of the supplies from the nearby Tennessee town of Tiptonville.[21] This condition indicated in one way the approaching end of this era and the beginning of a new one for Kentucky Bend.

Calling Out An Order Of Hay

Endnotes

1. This ferry service progressed from the use of various types of skiffs, carrying only passengers, through wooden and then steel barges serving wagons and coaches in addition to passengers, and finally different-sized gas-powered ferries later adding cars and trucks to their fare and operating on a regular schedule. Personal interview with George Franklin.

2. Personal interview with E.F. Wadley.

3. Personal interview with E.A. Peacock.

4. Portions of the account follow: "There's been more than one feud around here, in old times, but I reckon the first one was between the Darnells and the Watsons . . . . Both families belonged to the same church (everybody around here is religious); through all of this fifty or sixty years' fuss, both tribes was there every Sunday, to worship. They lived each side of the line, and the church was at a landing called Compromise. Half the church and half the aisle was in Kentucky, the other half in Tennessee. Sundays you'd see the families drive up, all in their Sunday clothes - men, women, and children - and file up the aisle, and sit down quietly and orderly, one lot on the Tennessee side of the Church and the other on the Kentucky side . . ." Samuel L. Clemens, Life on the *Mississippi* (New York, 1956; orig. pub. 1883), 219-21.

5. Personal interview with George P. Hopson.

6. *Statistics of the Population of the United States at the Tenth Census (June 1, 1880),* I, 188.

7. *Report of Population of the United States at the Eleventh Census: 1890,* Part I, 160.

8. Herbert and Edward Zuick, *Mississippi Steamboating* (New York, 1926), 257.

9. Louis C. Hunter, *Steamboats on the Western Rivers* (Cambridge, Mass., 1949), 346.

10. The latter was located at the northern tip of the Bend. Personal interview with J.L. Decker.

11. Mississippi River Landings (in the Kentucky Bend area) between Cairo and New Orleans:

(Distances from Cairo)	
Kentucky and Tennessee state line	63
Morrisons Landing, Missouri	69
Watson's Point, Kentucky	69
New Madrid, Missouri	70
Lower Madrid Landing, Missouri	71
Nolands Landing, Kentucky	75
Toney Landing, Missouri	75
Marrs Landing, Tennessee	77

Henry G. Adams, *Report on Transportation Business in the United States at the Eleventh Census of the United States 1890,* XIV, Part 2 (Transportation by Walter), 421.

12. Personal interview with J.L. Decker.

13. Personal interview with E.F. Wadley.

14. *Ibid.*

15. Personal interview with J.L. Decker.

16. Personal interview with George R. Hopson.

17. Personal interview wih J.L. Decker.

18. George Tipton Wilson, "Ol' Man River's Bender," *Nashville Tennessean Magazine*, Jan. 4, 1953.

19. Personal interview with J.L. Decker.

20. Personal interview with E.F. Wadley.

21. Testimony of William Columbus Gunnels contained in records of the *Whitson vs. Morris* lawsuit made available by C. King Davis.

"Kentucky Bend - The Lock That Had to be Released," by Allen Anthony, is reprinted from *The Register Of The Kentucky Historical Society,* ©1979, Volume 77, No. 2 (Spring 1979), pp. 108-111, by permission of The Kentucky Historical Society.

3C

Kentucky Bend - The Lock That Had To Be Released

Kentucky Bend,[1] the isolated portion of Fulton County, Kentucky, was granted a definite boundary (Fig. 1) with the state of Tennessee just in time to find itself situated shortly thereafter in the middle of a crucial region of contention during the Civil War. The location within the bend of the Mississippi River suddenly became more significant than perhaps ever before to the inhabitants of the Bend. This river, says Zuick, "was the highway over which the sinews of war must be transported to the front. It was the gateway to the agricultural wealth of the South."[2] If the Mississippi therefore was the doorway, then Island No. 10 was surely the knob that had to be grasped. But before this could be done, Kentucky Bend was the lock that had to be released (Fig. 2). Historians generally seem to contend that once Union gunboats slipped past Island No. 10 and reached New Madrid, Missouri, the eventual loss of that strategic island by Confederate forces was a foregone conclusion. However, the actual landing of Union troops on the Kentucky Bend shoreline was required to force the abandonment of Island No. 10 and the adjoining Tennessee shoreline by the Confederates.

When Union forces earlier had advanced to the outskirts of New Madrid, the Confederate forces evacuated and escaped across the Mississippi River to Kentucky Bend where, military correspondence reveals, they "scattered in the wide bottoms."[3]

Records of both forces give conflicting viewpoints of advantage and optimism in this area, while revealing, in respective proposals, plans either for capturing or holding the strategic Kentucky Bend. Major General John Pope, commanding Union forces at New Madrid and realizing the danger of attempting a landing, felt that unless this was done, military operations against Island No. 10 would have to be abandoned.[4] He had outlined a plan for invasion[5] which would not require the assistance of Union gunboats then blocked above Island No. 10. Confederate officer E.D. Blake, though realizing the possibility of the enemy's slipping by under the cover of night, still felt he had the advantages of high water, favorable shoreline conditions on the northern tip of the Bend, and battery defenses in areas where landings were possible.[6]

The peninsula, so-called, opposite New Madrid was described at that particular time as being actually an island. This was based on the report that Kentucky Bend, along with the remainder of the area within the loop, was surrounded on three sides by the Mississippi River and on the fourth by the flooded channel, comprised of Reelfoot Lake and low inundated swampland rejoining the Mississippi below Tiptonville.[7]

Although the shoreline reportedly was lined with batteries to prevent passage of the river by the Union forces,[8] darkness enabled two gunboats, the *Caron-*

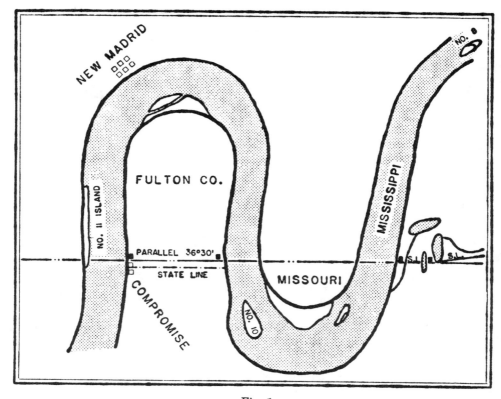

Fig. 1

SOURCE: The Report of the Boundary Line Commissioners of Kentucky and Tennessee to the Honorable Isham G. Harris, Governor of Tennessee - November 11, 1859.

delet and the *Pittsburgh*, to slip by or at least to survive the venture and arrive safely on April 4 and 6, respectively, 1862, at New Madrid for use in observing and shelling the defensive batteries on the west side of Kentucky Bend in preparation for the planned landing. Troop strength at New Madrid had been greatly increased by the arrival of boats through the hastily constructed canal through flooded swamps in Missouri above Island No. 10, which permitted Union forces to get from the Mississippi River above the Confederate fortifications across to Pope's command at New Madrid.[9]

The stage was now set for the invasion of Kentucky Bend. Reports stated that the forces stationed on the Bend, a portion of the seven thousand men in the greater area of the river's loop, were ready to defend its banks. Early on the morning of April 7, both gunboats proceeded downstream to Watson's Landing, the point selected for the landing of troops, where they were joined by the Union shore batteries in firing on the Confederate batteries there located (Fig. 4). By twelve o'clock, the Watson Landing weapons had been silenced. Thereupon, Pope issued the signal which caused steamers carrying Brigadier General E.A.

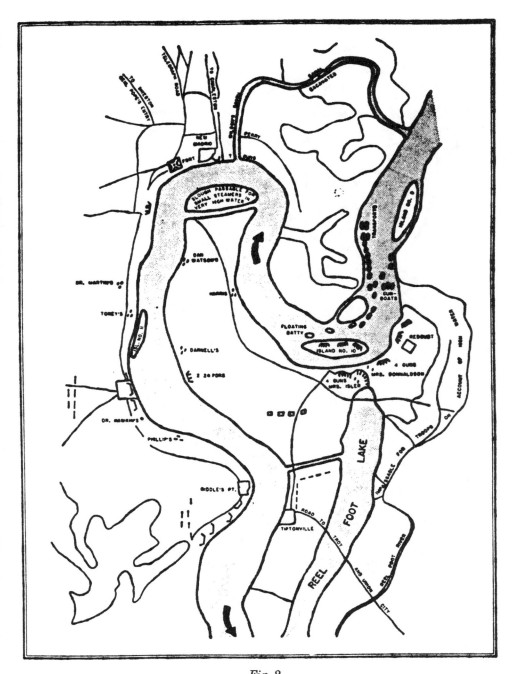

Fig. 2

SOURCE: Confederate fortifications on the Mississippi River at Island No. 10 and New Madrid. Plate 10, Atlas to accompany to official records of the Union and Confederate Armies.

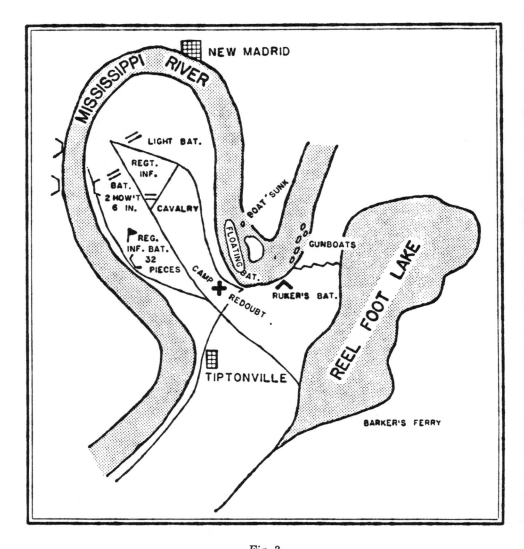

Fig. 3

SOURCE: A map enclosed in Report of Lt. E.D. Blake, CSA, dated April 10, 1862, ad-dressed to Maj. Gen. L. Polk, Commander First Corps, Army of Mississippi. O.R., Series I, Volume VII.

Attack At Watson's Landing

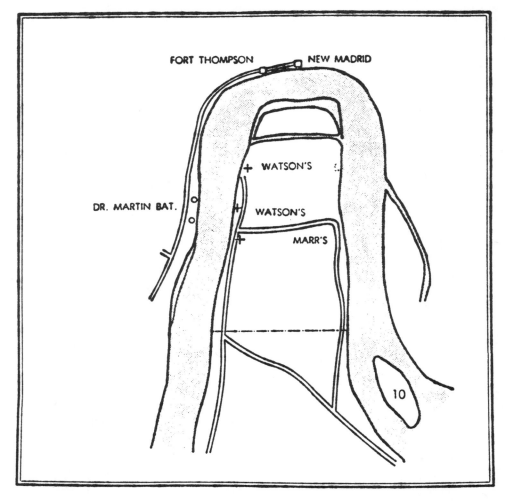

Fig. 4

<table>
<tr><td>+</td><td>**CONFEDERATE STATES BATTERIES**</td></tr>
<tr><td>O</td><td>**FEDERAL BATTERIES**</td></tr>
</table>

From the original for General P.
G. T. Beauregard, in
O.R., Series I, Volume VIII.

Paine's division to head out as planned. (These steamers earlier in the morning had been brought from the canal and loaded with Union troops.)[10]

Thus on April 7, 1862, the enemy "with a large army" crossed the "wide furious river" to invade Kentucky Bend.[11] As the steamers approached Watson's Landing, the Confederate forces foresaw their fate and began a hasty withdrawal and apparently a disorganized retreat. When this news was delivered to Pope by a spy, the general stopped Paine, notified him of the situation, and gave orders "to land as rapidly as possible on the opposite shore and push forward to Tiptonville to which point the enemy's forces were tending from every direction."[12]

The Union troops were landed at Watson's Landing[13] as planned, and by that midnight the entire force had been brought down and across the river to the landing and were "pushing forward rapidly" after the fleeing enemy.[14]

Hence the retreat and chase continued southward out of Kentucky Bend. Island No. 10 likewise had been abandoned. The result was a rout and a mass surrender by the Confederate forces trapped on this "temporary island." Kentucky Bend passed from Confederate to Union occupation.

Compromise (Fig. 1) was the scene of one of the battles of the Civil War and later "crumbled into the river," according to one writer.[15] Little is recorded concerning the life of the local inhabitants or of incidents involving particular places within the Bend during this period of turmoil, with the exception of one atrocity inflicted upon the members of a local family. In a sense, Kentucky Bend was more peculiarly important to the Civil War than was the Civil War to Kentucky Bend.

Endnotes

1. The term Kentucky Bend is confined today to that state's part of the larger loop of the Mississippi River known variously as Madrid Bend, New Madrid Bend, or Bessie Bend. Early maps, including those prepared during the Civil War, often failed to show a state boundary line to distinguish the Kentucky portion from the remainder of the greater bend located in Tennessee. Writings, including Civil War reports, often awarded the entire area within the loop to Tennessee. The focus of this study will be limited to the smaller area now known as Kentucky Bend.

2. Herbert and Edward Zuick, *Mississippi Steamboating* (New York, 1926), 264.

3. John Pope to G.W. Cullum, March 14, 1862, *The War of the Rebellion: A Compilation of the Official Records of the Union and Confederate Armies* (128 vols., Washington, D.C., 1880-1901), Series I, Vol. VIII, 83.

4. *Ibid.*

5. Pope planned to "tow one or two of these batteries [barges protected by cottonwood rails and cotton bales] over the river to a point exactly opposite New Madrid, where swamps prevented any access to the river and where the enemy therefore, had been unable to establish his batteries. When near the shore the

floating batteries, with their crews, were to be cut loose from the steamers and allowed to float down the river to the point selected for landing the troops . . . ." *Ibid.*, 87-88.

6. Blake wrote that unless the enemy can pass "in front of our batterries in the obscurity of some stormy night . . . the high water may prove a successful barrier against the enemy's efforts to obtain a foothold in the bend. On the east Reelfoot Lake is impassable to either flats or rafts. Between the batteries and the point marked A on the annexed map (Fig. 3) it is impossible for him to cross with steam power. Between A and B the country is submerged, and does not admit of a landing. Between B and Tiptonville flats may be landed; but a few batteries judiciously planted on the shore could effectually prevent a disembarkation . . . It seems to be certain then, that unless the enemy can put boats below the Madrid batteries the forces at Island No. 10 and Madrid Bend are secure against assault until the water falls at least five feet, and even a few guns could prevent a landing." *Ibid.*, 136.

7. *Ibid.*, 85.

8. *Ibid.*, 78.

9. *Ibid.*, 88.

10. *Ibid.*, 88-90.

11. *Ibid.*, 78.

12. *Ibid.*, 89.

13. Although definite boundaries were established at this time, military correspondence reveals an evident lack of knowledge of state lines in the area. Reference is made to Watson's Landing as being on the Tennessee shore. *Ibid.*, 118.

14. *Ibid.*, 89.

15. Onida Jewell, "A River Finds Mystery - and Madrid Bend is Born," *Fulton* [Ky.] *News*, Oct. 12, 1951.

"Reverie: A Tennessee Post Office in a Disabled Arkansas School Bus" is taken from "Two Tennessee Communities That 'Crossed' the Mississippi River: Displacement and Isolation as Factors in Folklife," by Allen Anthony, and is reprinted from *Kentucky Folklore Record: A Regional Journal Of Folklore and Folklife,* Volume 29, No. 3 and 4 (July-December 1983), pp. 50-71, by permission.

4

REVERIE, TENNESSEE

Reverie: A Tennessee Post Office In A Disabled Arkansas School Bus

In 1819 the original Shelby County was established from the recently acquired Jackson Purchase which provided what is known today as West Tennessee. Four years later, from this initial county which occupied a large portion of the southwestern corner of the region, Tipton County was created. This new county, located in the northwestern part of its matrix, had the Mississippi River as its western boundary and therein gained ownership of several islands lying near the Tennessee shoreline. Two of these, Island No. 35 and Island No. 37, served as area settings for the later establishment respectively of the communities of Reverie and Corona, rural settlements which presently find themselves isolated across the river on the Arkansas side. The final chapters are concerned with the establishment and survival of these unusual communities, and the factors of physical displacement and resulting isolation from the Tennessee mainland are examined in terms of their effect upon the folklife of these inhabitants (Fig. 1).

The settlement of Island No. 35 occurred in 1849, and George Pennel and Jerry Epps were two of its original residents. Epps lived until 1950 when he died at the age of 106.[1] The main channel of the river at the time of the island's initial occupance, and for many decades thereafter, was located off the northwestern or Arkansas side of Island No. 35 (Fig. 2). Only a relatively narrow and shallow slough actually separated the island from the Tennessee mainland during the early years. In highwater stage some steamboats on occasions would attempt a shortcut through this risky passageway. While some steamers succeeded, one did not; the *Emma III* mired and sank in this chute in 1870. According to one account, the inhabitants of the island "dug into the mud-filled wreckage and salvaged the silverware and dishes." These residents reportedly treasured the recovered items as least well into the next century, and one family, later quite prominent on the island, was to take great pride in retaining the boat's bell.[2]

As the number of inhabitants on Island No. 35 continued to increase, the need for postal service eventually was recognized. In 1875 the Reverie Post Office, named by the U.S. Post Office Department in Washington, D.C.,[3] was established at a steamboat landing[4] located, according to one early map, near the lower or downstream end of the island along the main channel of the river, but according to later more reliable maps, nearer the upstream end of the island. It is likely that steamers stopped at other landings along the island's edge as would

97

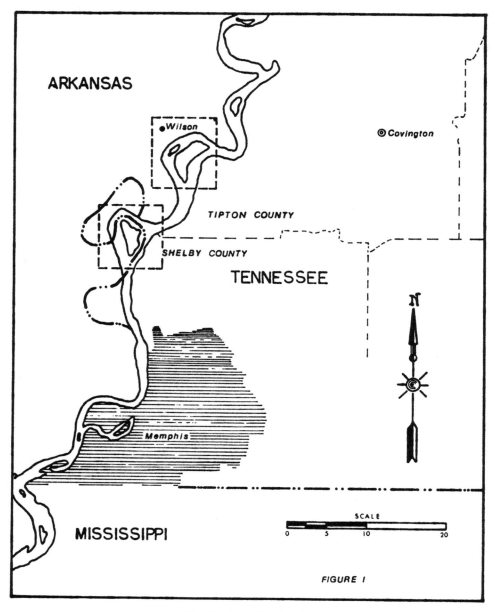

Fig. 1 - Area For Study

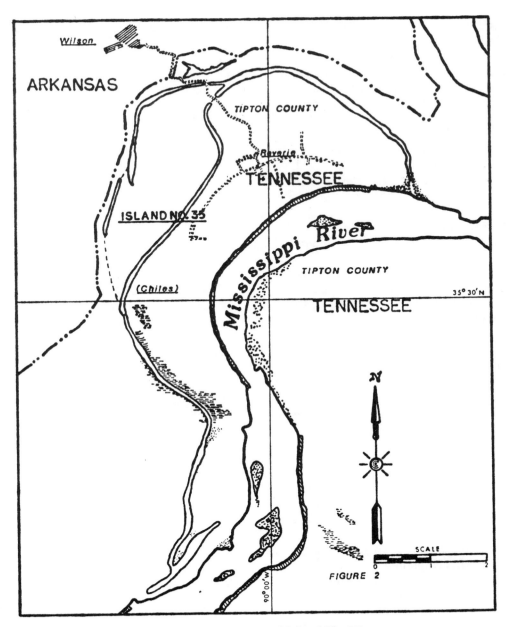

Fig. 2 - Reverie and Island No. 35
Adapted from map entitled "Map No. 12, Lower Mississippi River," Mississippi River
Commission, in collection of the U.S. Corps of Engineers, Memphis, Tennessee, 1979.

have been the practice during delivering and picking up different supplies and products.

From the post office's identification came the designation of Reverie Landing and the beginning of the community which was to bear its name. The landing became a leading stopping point for steamboats and packets. Mrs. Ora Cash, a matriarch for one of the leading families on the island, remembered visits of such well-known vessels as the *Robert E. Lee* and the *Fred Herald*. She later recalled, "The big sternwheelers used to tie up at Pennel Brothers General Store. The whole town turned out. The youngsters were thrilled and wide-eyed by the shrill whistle."[5]

During the late 1800s and the first decade of the 1900s an interesting practice took place on the island. Refined and educated women arrived by steamboat, boarded in the homes of some of the leading families, and there taught the children music and other subjects from the classics.[6]

By 1892 the land area of Island No. 35, even though still heavily forested in the interior, was rather well occupied or at least title to property was widely established. A dozen different names can be identified on a map. Reverie had tri-weekly mail service by that time and J.W. Pennel was the postmaster. Other leading citizens were H.H. Clifton, a lawyer; J.B. Ewet, a physician; and William Wright, a carpenter. The Pennel brothers operated a cotton gin.[7]

In the early years of the new century, perhaps the beginning of the heyday for Reverie and Island No. 35, the insular population was reported to have been about 750, representing approximately 300 families.[8] A long-time resident recently estimated the local count in 1912 to have numbered about 800 people. Prominent individuals recalled from this era include Dan Needam and Emmet Chiles. The latter was affectionately known as "Doctor Chiles," though the title was not based upon a medical diploma but instead on his practice of "doctoring people" by dispensing patent medicine and other supplies along with free "home-remedy" advice from a store which he operated near one of the landings.[9]

Before 1920 during low-water stages each year, the slough separating Island No. 35 from the mainland on the Tennessee side was still narrow enough and the water so shallow on these occasions that horse-and-buggy units were able to cross back and forth.[10] It was reported that under such circumstances an islander "could ford The Slough and drive a buggy through the cotton fields to Covington, the county seat, in two hours."[11]

At this time, however, the main channel of the Mississippi River was cutting into the Tennessee side farther upstream where a bluff eventually disappeared. This widened sweep made it possible for the current to begin a frontal attack on the upriver entrance to the slough. As a result, the slough began to widen and deepen. The U.S. Engineers attempted to block this action of the river by constructing an earthen dam along the head of the island during the early 1920s.[12]

A ferry, operated by Joe Whitson, provided service for a number of years between the head of the island and a point on the mainland known as Richardson Landing. This operation ended about 1925 or 1926.[13]

Crossing by Buggy in the Shallow Channel

During the 1920s and the early 1930s a number of business and other social institutions provided goods and services to Reverie and the remainder of the island. The various facilities available to the inhabitants during at least a part of this period included three 8-grade schools (one on the head of the island, another in the middle - for the "colored" - and a third on the foot of the island), two or three churches (again one for the "colored"), two general merchandise stores (the one near the middle of the island at Reverie contained the post office at that time), and two cotton gins.[14]

In 1927 one of the major floods of the century inundated low-lying areas of the Mississippi floodplain. All but three spots on Island No.35 were covered by the floodwaters. Until the water receded, all the residents then on the island stayed "in a schoolhouse, a house and a barn on one of the mounds. A large flock of ducks laid eggs every night on top of the schoolhouse, so there were fresh eggs for breakfast every morning."[15]

The flood of 1927 did more than bring losses and inconveniences to the inhabitants of Reverie and its island. The high water apparently strained the capacity of the sloughs as it then existed, according to one local authority, and marked the beginning of the river channel's shift from the Arkansas side of the island to the Tennessee side.[16] Clearly the main channel separated Island No. 35 from the Tennessee mainland by the early 1930s. Much fertile farmland was lost along the side of the island in the process, especially from the property belonging to the Cash family, a leading landowner.[17]

With the shift of the channel to the Tennessee side of the island, the old river course began its transition to an abandoned channel and eventually a slough along the Arkansas shoreline. Within a short time the original Reverie Landing lost its advantage as a location about midway on the northwestern side of the island. Soon the steamboats began to stop at a landing near the foot of the island to load and unload the mail and other cargo. The mail sacks were carried by horseback between this point and the post office which remained in the store at Reverie. In time the exchange of mail was made at a landing near the head of the island, where once again the appointed horse rider made a round trip from the Reverie post office. The sound of the boat's distinct whistle as the vessel approached the old landing at the lower end of the island from its earlier Memphis dispatch gave the mailbag carrier and others meeting the boat time to hurry to the upper landing.[18] Another landing during this time was established just upstream to load and unload cargo.[19]

The record high water of the great flood of 1937 covered the entire island, but some members of the Cash family stayed in their home, taking refuge in the upstairs' floor. It was reported the "Boats came to the second story window."[20] But the waters, as before, did recede. The residents of Island No. 35 recovered from the damage inflicted and life returned to normal.

Reverie inhabitants and other island neighbors during this time established a reputation as concerned and participating voters in their local precinct, despite their separation and resulting isolation from the remainder of the larger "mother" county of which their island was a part. One resident, Horace Phelan Cash, the patriarch of this leading family, was elected to the United States House of Representatives where he served during the 1940s.[21]

The river which isolated it could be both friend and foe. It provided the artery upon which steamboats could in a sense bring the world to the door of Island No. 35 through its landings. The occasional overflow of its flood waters, while inflicting some damage, brought the overlay of enriching silt to the fields of the island. The river could also "play tricks" on the island's inhabitants by creating uncertainty at times over the years as to which side of the island it wished its main channel to pass by on. On occasions, which fortunately were infrequent, it could take its toll of human life from those who had to cross its surface going back and forth between the island and the mainland on either side.

One such instance of the danger of the Mississippi occurred early in 1949 about dusk on a cold January evening. The water surface of the new slough, now the narrow passage separating Island No. 35 from the Arkansas shoreline, was rough. Two women and a man were returning from a funeral on the Arkansas mainland by boat to Reverie, their home town. The women were the local school teachers. Something went wrong before they reached the opposite shore, and all three perished.[22]

By the early 1950s there still were no utility-provided systems on the island to furnish electricity, water, or telephone service. Life still moved at a rather leisurely pace in a setting of isolation and unavailability of many modern conveniences then taken for granted on the mainland. Residents felt there was no other place in the South where the pace of life so nearly approached that of the beginning of the century. With farm mechanization the population of Island No. 35 had decreased to approximately 300 inhabitants.[23]

A noteworthy exception to the rather simple if not austere lifestyle of most residents of the Reverie community was the home of the Cash family. This modern, fine house, as judged by local standards of that time, contained eight rooms and was the largest residence on the island. It was built in 1936 and erected at a height of seven feet above the ground to permit a safety margin for high water during flood periods. The house was constructed of lumber secured from trees growing on the island and the ceilings and walls were paneled in walnut and oak.[24] While other homes on the island were lighted by kerosene at that time, the Cash residence had a "private electric-generating system" which provided electric lights for both the livingroom and kitchen. Kerosene lamps were used in the other rooms. A television set was located in the livingroom. Most of the pieces of furniture in the home were over a century old by then.[25]

Horace P. Cash, the "leading citizen" of Reverie for many years, had died by this time. His widow, Mrs. Ora Cash, now was the "island matriarch." She had lived most of her life on Island No. 35 and was quoted as saying she "wouldn't leave for anything."[26] Her oldest son, Phelan, then was the owner of an unpainted, wood general store which provided such merchandise as groceries, hardware and clothing for the community's residents. This was the only business establishment on the island at this time.[27] Phelan Cash maintained a home in Reverie, but his primary residence was now in nearby Wilson, Arkansas, across the slough on the mainland where his children attended school.[28] At this time a small ferry provided service between the island and the Arkansas shoreline near Wilson.[29]

Cash, fellow island resident W.T. Carr, and J.E.Crain of Wilson then were the owners of most of the fertile farmland and timber resources on the island. Cash and Crain at that time were the local magistrates of the quarterly court of Tipton County, Tennessee having jurisdiction on Island No. 35.[30] Court trials were held in the open under a large old tree in Reverie.[31]

The little red schoolhouse, the only one left on the island by then, served a total of ninety-six pupils in classes through the eighth grade. The teachers were the Reverend and Mrs. Eldon Cornett. He also served as the pastor of the Nazarene

The Cash home [1952]   *Mrs. Cash lights a lamp [1952]*

Reprint from article photocopy as only available source
Permission of The Commercial Appeal

"Aunt Mildred"   *The spreading*   *Phelans Cash's*   *The school*
Craig   *pecan tree*   *Store*

[1940]

Reprint from article photocopy as only available source
Permission of The Commercial Appeal

Church, the only house of worship remaining on Island No. 35 at that time.[32] Before the decade ended that last church on Island No. 35 had closed when its minister left to live in Memphis. The school did not reopen in 1957 because no teacher was available.[33] The building was described as "abandoned" in 1958.[34]

Reports differed during this time concerning the degree of tranquility and the extent of law and order on the island. An article in an area newspaper in 1957 stated that, since it was another Saturday night on Island No. 35, violence flared as usual. A resident of Osceola, located further upstream in Arkansas, contended that "things like that go on all the time over there' and 'it would take Wyatt Earp himself to go over there and clean them out."[35]

The Arkansan provided details that included a pistol-whipping, a pistol being drawn on another victim whose life was threatened in a local honky tonk, and a beating during the previous month of a man with a sawmill pulley belt. Though there was a constable living on the island, an official in the sheriff's department on the other side of the river in Covington, Tennessee, having jurisdiction over all of Tipton County, reported that office did not know anything about such incidents and that there had been no arrests or even reports of violence. The Tipton County sheriff, or his deputy, if needed would have had to travel south to Memphis to cross a bridge and then return north on the Arkansas side to gain access to Island No. 35.[36] An Arkansan observer, noting that after all the island was on the Arkansas side of the river, complained, "'I can't see why Arkansas shouldn't have jurisdiction on Island 35.'"[37]

In 1960 the first bridge was erected across the narrowing slough to connect the island with the Arkansas shoreline near the town of Wilson.[38] This new link, built with Tennessee highway funding, displaced the ferry operation. It was of course welcomed but was at best a narrow and rather unstable structure.

In 1960 also came another high-level flood to Island No. 35. A previous resident of Reverie returned to the community on a boat "while the water was still up" to survey the damage. He anticipated finding the inhabitants contributing their tears to the overflowing murky Mississippi. The cotton crop was entirely ruined, and most of the soybeans were destroyed. But he was surprised at the spirit and behavior of the area residents, as shown in his description:

> You know what they were doing?. . . They were out there water-skiing in the cotton fields! They had three boats, and everybody took turns. The men would drive while the women skied, and then the women would drive.[39]

By 1967 Island No. 35 was described as being "cresent-shaped about ten miles long and five wide, with concrete revetments on its eastern lip to keep the river from biting deeper."[40] Reverie was then estimated to be located nearly a mile from the Tennessee mainland. Across the slough between the island and the Arkansas side, the recently-built wooden bridge, shifting on its support poles in the soft mud and resembling "a snake on a hot rock," did little to attract prospective visitors during the latter part of that decade. Two individuals had driven off the bridge and the states of Tennessee and Arkansas were locked in a jurisdictional dispute over which state was the site of the drownings.[41] Fear of losses from repeated flooding and the displacement of field laborers resulting from mechanized farming operations combined to reduce the island's population to thirty families, or approximately 125 residents. The landscape was now dotted with deserted houses. The only landowners still living on the island were the John and H.P. Cash families which were headed by the sons of the matriarch, Ora Cash. These families at that time cultivated about 6,000 acres on the island. The remainder of the land, more than half of the total, was then owned by absentee landlords and tilled by resident managers.[42]

In 1967 the distance, "as the crow flies," from Reverie to its county seat of Covington on the mainland was still about twenty miles. But travel by road required a trip of approximately two hours by crossing the Mississippi River either

The bridge to Reverie: It crosses The Slough like a nervous snake [1967]

The island's soil is deep and rich, and farming is almost completely mechanized [1967]

Many years ago, court trials were held under this old tree in Reverrie [1967]

"Main Street" in Reverie [1967]

Mrs. Ora Cash: Matriarch of the Cashes of Reverie [1967]

©Robert E. Kollar

Courtesy of Robert E. Kollar

Permission of The Nashville Tennessean

From the east bank of Island 35, the people of Reverie can see the Tennessee mainland nearly a mile away across the waters of the Mississippi [1967]

by bridge at Memphis to the south or by ferry at Cottonwood Point, Missouri to the north.[43] The isolation from the remainder of the island's county and state, as well as separation from the Arkansas shoreline resulting from the narrowing but still formidable slough crossable only by a rather precarious wooden bridge, resulted in a continuing condition of remoteness and even resistance to change at this late date in the century.

The island still had no law enforcement officer any closer than the circuitous route required from Covington. Reverie no longer had a general store or even a little grocery to provide the local residents with basic food items. When the bridge to the Arkansas shore was covered by occasional flood waters, medical emergencies could occur, and a few deaths resulting from ruptured appendices were recalled by inhabitants.

On election day voting took place on the front porch of the home of the local county magistrate, John Cash. This official reported that at least ninety percent of the registered voters in the precinct cast their ballots regularly and by generally voting as a solid block they "carry a little weight." When a contest was close, there was "nailbiting in Covington" until the ballot box -always the last to arrive - was received.[44]

During each spring when on several occasions the bridge was under water, the thirty-eight Reverie school children had to be taken across the slough on a boat to board the school bus on the Arkansas side for the ride to nearby Wilson schools. They attended the Wilson schools through an arrangement between the Arkansas officials and the school board in Tipton County, Tennessee, which had authority over and was responsible for educational provisions involving school-aged children on Island No. 35.[45]

The mail came to Reverie each Monday, Wednesday, and Friday. On these three days Wanda Lee Cash, the wife of H.P. Cash, served as postmistress for the community. Patrons simply came to a little window on the front porch of her home where they rang a school bell to secure service.

By this time there was electricity from an Arkansas utility available on the island to provide power for washing machines, air conditioners, television sets, and other household needs for residents who wanted and could afford such modern conveniences. But the proposed extension of telephone service to Reverie from the neighboring state was refused at that time as a threat of too much progress, or at least a potential nuisance. John Cash said, "if my brother or I had a phone, everyone on the island would want to use it and we'd be taking calls at all hours of the day and night. It's just not worth it."[46]

In 1974 farmers of the community, tired of waiting for financial assistance to be provided to restore the old wooden bridge which had since collapsed, built a dike across the slough supporting a road to reestablish the link with the Arkansas mainland. But two years later the Mississippi River at flood stage caused the level of the slough to rise sharply and wash away the new dike, once again isolating the island's population of about 100 except for small boat operations. During this time approximately thirteen students were thus transported the 400 feet each way to and from the Arkansas bank to permit them to maintain

Cash picks up the mail from postmistress Wanda Lee Cash, his sister-in-law [1967]

their school attendance. Tennessee officials reportedly began to search for a way to secure financing for a new bridge, while Reverie residents were not optimistic about chances for an early replacement of their lost span.[47] In time the link was reestablished with a more stable, concrete bridge. Thus, at present, with the exception of occasional high-water stages, the inhabitants of Island No. 35 appear to have a safe and dependable roadway between Reverie, Tennessee and Wilson, Arkansas.

Today about twenty-two families, or between eighty and ninety people, live on this island on the "wrong" side of the Mississippi River. Essentially all the land is farmed, but mechanization has lessened the need for farm laborers. In the sense of service provisions, Island No. 35 seems to "belong to" both states. In addition to providing school and store facilities, Arkansas utilities and distributors have extended not only electricity but also bottled gas to the Reverie community. The residents continue to refuse the offer of telephone service as either unnecessary or bothersome. Mail service, though utilizing a Tennessee ZIP code, is extended through the Wilson post office. A school bus on a route out of Wilson now picks up and returns approximately thirty students on days when school is operating and the bridge is passable.

The state of Tennessee at the county level provides basic government services to this outpost. The highway department makes a road grader available for seasonal use. A sheriff's deputy can be dispatched from Covington to make the still-lengthy round trip when necessary after a request is received either by phone from Wilson or, more recently, by CB radio from Reverie. Tipton County election officials still eagerly await on voting day those last results in the box from the distant Fourteenth District on Island No. 35. An early election talley is now reported by phone from Wilson before the box arrives in Covington.[48]

Some years ago the post office operation on the island was moved from the old Cash home to a nearby, separate building erected especially for that purpose. In 1977 that facility burned and the service was returned briefly to the Cash home.[49] Mrs. Marie Cash, who has been the postmaster at Reverie for about twelve years now, continues the chain of members of the Cash family who have served in that position since a post office was first established on the island in 1875.[50] She quickly contacted the Wilson school system and was successful in obtaining a school bus which had become inoperative when the engine was destroyed by fire.[51] Thus Reverie obtained a new post office. The postmistress arranged for an appropriate exterior trim of red, white and blue, provided the renovation of the bus's interior, "complete with desk, scales and all the necessary postal equipment," as well as a sofa for patrons awaiting service, and then opened for business. She provides service each work day afternoon from 3:00 p.m. to 6:00 p.m.[52] after completing her morning work as a school lunchroom employee in Wilson where she now maintains a home.[53]

The river, of course, still threatens with its periodic rises. Recently the water lacked only four inches of reaching the floor level of the blocked-up post office. But the islanders seem to take such occurrences in stride. Each family maintains a motor boat, and "they catch a lot of catfish when the water is up and they

114

River Waters Engulf Long-Abandoned Bus; Students Now Travel By Boat [1982]

Photo by Ron Russell

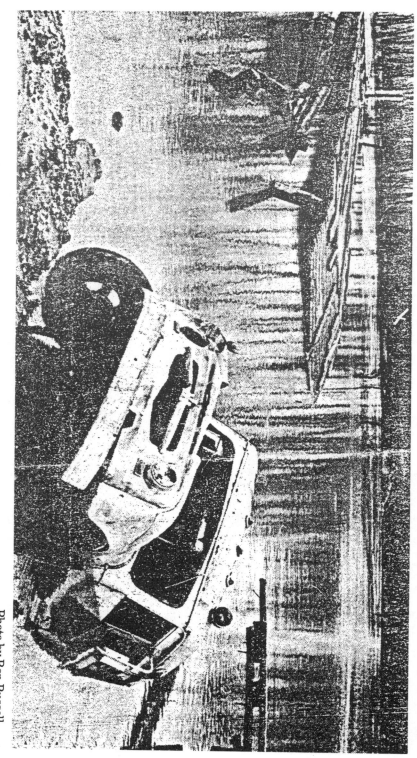

Road Leading To Tennessee's Island 35 Was Washed Out Two Weeks Ago And Residents Remain Isolated [1982]

Photo by Ron Russell
Reprint from article photocopy as only available source
Permission of The Commercial Appeal

Photo by Thomas Busler
A school bus unloads children on the far side of Reverie's washed-out road. [1982]
Reprint from article photocopy as only available source
Permission of The Commercial Appeal

Road Over Bridge Between Wilson, Arkansas and Reverie/Island No. 35, Tennessee
Courtesy of Thomas H. Anthony

Recent View of Reverie on Island No. 35
Courtesy of Thomas H. Anthony

School Bus Post Office at Reverie
Courtesy of Thomas H. Anthony

Reverie Post Office
...Marie Cash, postmaster [1979]
Reprint from article photocopy as only available source
Permission of The Covington Leader

Photo by Thomas Busler

Some Residents Commute To Arkansas In Boats [1982]
Reprint from article photocopy as only available source
Permission of The Commercial Appeal

Photo by Thomas Busler
Marie Cash brings mail by boat to Reverie.
Reprint from article photocopy as only
available source
Permission of The Commercial Appeal

can't do anything else."[54] During such times when the bridge is under water, school attendance by the children is not interrupted. The fathers in a fleet of approximately fourteen motor boats deliver their children across the flooded slough to the bus on the Arkansas side each morning and return to pick up their passengers in the afternoon. Mail service also is maintained by motor boat operation under these circumstances.[55] Over 100 years after Reverie was first established on Island No. 35, then located on the Tennessee side of the Mississippi River, as Mrs. Cash concludes, the misplaced Tennesseans "have an exciting life."[56]

A FINAL GLIMPSE

A recent inquiry reveals that there was a development not long ago that has affected the lives of the people residing on Island No. 35. Mrs. Marie Cash retired as postmaster at Reverie on May 31, 1984. At that time the United States Postal Service terminated all services offered through the school bus post office located in that little community. Although some of the island's residents had already begun to drive to nearby Wilson, Arkansas to pick up their mail at that town's full-service facility, all inhabitants desiring postal services must now make this trip. There is no rural route service to the attached island. The era of local mail service apparently had come to a close. Otherwise, life in the Reverie area continues much the same.[57]

Endnotes

1. Agnes Fite, "The Story of a Little Island in a Big River," *Press-Scimitar* (Memphis), 19 August 1952.

2. Bob Kollar, "Between the River and The Slough," *Nashville Tennessean, Parade,* 23 July 1967.

3. Carolyn Smith, ed., "Mail Must Go Through," *Covington Leader*, 27 June 1979.

4. "Reverie, Tennessee Mail Goes Through Arkansas," *Mail Call*, Memphis, Tennessee Sectional Center, Main Post Office, Memphis, Tennessee, (August 1979): 2.

5. Kollar.

6. Wilbur Cash, interview with author, Covington, Tennessee, 13 May 1980.

7. *Tennessee State Gazetteer and Business Directory*. (Memphis: R.L. Polk and Company, 1890-1891), 709.

8. Kollar.

9. Mrs. Lizzie Godsey and Mrs. Marie Cash, interview with author, Island No. 35, Tennessee, 11 May 1980.

10. W. Cash, interview.

11. Kollar.

12. *Ibid.*

13. W. Cash, interview; Wilbur Cash, letter to author, 15 January 1981.

14. M. Cash, interview; Marie Cash, letter to author, 31 August 1979.

15. Kollar.

16. W. Cash, interview.

17. Kollar.

18. Godsey and M. Cash, interview.

19. W. Cash, letter.

20. Kollar.

21. M. Cash, interview.

22. Kollar.
23. Fite.
24. *Ibid.*
25. *Ibid.*
26. *Ibid.*
27. *Ibid.*
28. *Ibid.*
29. Kollar.
30. Fite.
31. Kollar.
32. Fite.
33. *Press-Scimitar* (Memphis), 26 August 1957.
34. Kollar.
35. *Press-Scimitar.*
36. *Ibid.*
37. *Ibid.*
38. Kollar.
39. *Ibid.*
40. *Ibid.*
41. *Ibid.*
42. *Ibid.*
43. *Ibid.*
44. *Ibid.*
45. *Ibid.*
46. *Commercial Appeal* (Memphis), 9 March 1976.
47. Godsey and M. Cash, interview.
48. M. Cash, letter.
49. "Reverie, Tennessee Mail."
50. Godsey and M. Cash, interview.
51. Smith.
52. M. Cash, interview.
53. M. Cash, letter.
54. M. Cash, letter; M. Cash, interview.
55. M. Cash, letter.
56. Jan Taylor, "Bureaucracy Invades Island," *Commercial Appeal*, 21 July 1940.
57. M. Cash, telephone conversation with author, 2 October, 1984.

"Corona: From the Devil's Elbow to Centennial Island - Almost Overnight" is taken from "Two Tennessee Communities That 'Crossed' the Mississippi River: Displacement and Isolation as Factors in Folklife," by Allen Anthony, and is reprinted from *Kentucky Folklore Record: A Regional Journal Of Folklore and Folklife,* Volume 29, No. 3 and 4 (July-December 1983), pp. 50-71, by permission.

5

CORONA, TENNESSEE

Corona: From the Devil's Elbow To Centennial Island -- Almost Overnight

The community of Corona is associated with Island No. 37 primarily on the basis of proximity of the settlement to the island which lies within the same meander or loop of the river. Even though Island No. 36 may have been larger, or at least longer, than Island No. 37, likely predated its downstream neighbor, and was about as close to Corona when the latter was established, the former adhered to its shoreline following a channel change and later lost its identity as a point of reference for the community's location (Fig. 1).

Beyond evidence of early land grants in this bend, the ancestors of Sam S. Moore, who is apparently the community's leading citizen and spokesman today, have lived and farmed in the Corona area since 1836.[1] One of Moore's kinsmen, Walter S. Ulhorn, who lived in the vicinity recalled once that the property of this greater community had by 1940 been in the possession of his extended family for six generations. The original title holder to the land was John W. Trigg, at that time "one of the wealthiest men in this part of the South." Trigg Avenue in Memphis was later named for him.[2]

The exact date on which the name Corona was given to this settlement apparently has not yet been recorded in formal writing. Other early maps do not reveal any such appearance. Another member of the Moore clan, who with her husband also owns a home in the community, recalled that when her mother's family located in that area during the closing years of the Civil War, there was dissatisfaction with the label of Devil's Elbow then applied widely to the entire enclosure, perhaps with the exception of Island No. 37 and early steamboat landings, of this meander of the Mississippi. Thus the name Corona reportedly was first used for this small "family community" of perhaps two homes described as "sitting back in a grove." The site of the settlement was not far from the river's edge where was found, at that time, the landing which would bear the same name.[3] Therefore Corona at first likely was composed of two houses, a steamboat landing, and a post office operation.

Other than unhappiness with its prior identifications, the reason for giving the name Corona to this settlement is not found in printed accounts. The meaning of the word itself suggests a number of possible explanations. Since Corona at that time by best calculation or deduction was located near the northern-most "hump" or rounded extension of the mainland within the river's loop, Elizabeth

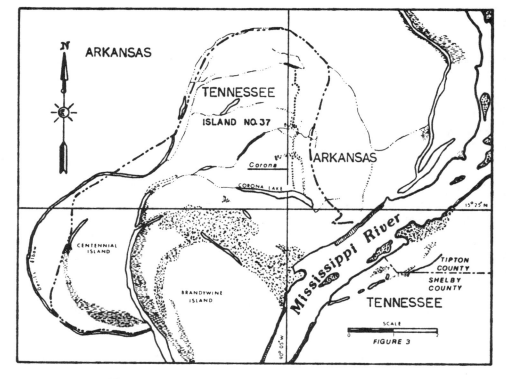

Fig. 1 - Corona, Centennial Island, and Island No. 37
Adapted from map entitled "Map No. 12, Lower Mississippi River," Mississippi River
Commission, in collection of the U.S. Corps of Engineers, Memphis, Tennessee, 1979.

Tipton suggests that the crown-like contour of the shoreline as it then existed
may well have been the inspiration for the community's new name.[4]

The first detailed map showing this area after Corona reportedly received its
name unfortunately does not acknowledge its appearance, either by its new label
or by any other designation. The notable work of Colonel Charles R. Suter, which
shows numerous other landings in the greater vicinity, fails to acknowledge a
landing for Corona. Corona and its surrounding area within the meander at this
time still had direct land connections with Covington, the county seat, and other
communities to the east of the bend's narrowing neck.

During this time the circuitous distance around the river's loop was reported
as thirty-five miles. Old-timers told of steamboat travelers who in those days
would disembark at the lower end of the bend at a point along the narrow passageway where they would spend most of the day visiting. Then they would cross
the "mile or so" to a landing on the upper end of the meander, apparently just

to the east of Corona, where the passengers reboarded their "delayed" boat to continue their upstream journey.[5]

Two years after Suter's map appeared a major occurrence took place during the country's centennial that was to have drastic and long-lasting effect on the Corona area. The *Supreme Court Reporter* vividly portrays the event in this account followed by portions of the court's decision in the noted case of *State of Arkansas v. State of Tennessee* decided in 1918:

> On March 7, 1876, the river suddenly and with great violence, within about thirty hours, made for itself a new channel directly across the neck opposite the apex of Dean's Island, so that the old channel around the bend of the elbow (a distance of fifteen to twenty miles) was abandoned by the current, and although it remained for a few years covered with dead water it was no longer navigable except in times of high water for small boats, and this continued only for a short time, since the old bed immediately began to fill with sand, sediment, and alluvial deposits. In the course of time it became dry land suitable for cultivation and to a considerable extent covered with timber. The new channel is called, from the year in which it originated, the 'Centennial Cut-Off,' and the land that separated from the Tennessee mainland goes by the name of 'Centennial Island.'
>
> (1) The true boundary line between the States, aside from the question of the avulsion of 1876, is the middle of the main channel of navigation as it existed at the Treaty of Peace concluded between the United States and Great Britain in 1783, subject to such changes as have occurred since that time through natural and gradual processes.
>
> (2) By the avulsion of 1876 the boundary line between the Stages was unaffected, and remained in the middle of the former main channel of navigation, as above defined.
>
> (3) The boundary line should now be located according to the middle of that channel as it was at the time the current ceased to flow therein as a result of the avulsion of 1876.[6]

The consequences of the brief rampage of nature therefore were significant for the area. The Mississippi had drastically shortened its course locally. The Centennial Cut-off had created Centennial Island, the former land area which had occupied the interior of the river's loop. Only Island No. 37 retained at this time its earlier identity. These two islands were now "cast off" and almost encircled by Arkansas. The channel of the old river would become the abandoned Barnay Cute while the passageway between Centennial Island and Island No. 37 would acquire the designation of McKenzie Chute. In time the water would largely disappear and soil materials would fill in most of the elongated depressions.

Clearly the community of Corona did not escape the effects of this alteration. The river, in making its cut across the neck at its narrowest point, swept through the "backyard" of the Corona settlement and took hundreds of acres of prime farmland from the fields which lay in the invader's path.[7] Nevertheless the community survived and reoriented itself near what then became the northeastern corner of the new Centennial Island and faced in a generally southeastwardly direction toward the new channel of the Mississippi. Corona was now isolated on the "wrong" side of the river. Its correct location in its new setting would not appear on forthcoming maps for many years.

The first such map to appear after this transformation of the greater area was published in 1878. Corona on this map appears to have been "washed" downstream and "deposited" just inland on the other or southeastern side of the river's new course. Seemingly, Corona had been returned to the Tennessee mainland! It is possible a corona of some identity could have been constituted and existed for a short period at that location, possibly as an "across-the-river" landing for a sandbar-blocked original Corona, as shown on several other later maps. Present-day landowners of the "real" settlement on Centennial Island, however, were amazed to hear of maps showing a Corona on the other side of the river and discounted any such possibility to the best of their knowledge.[8]

The map contained the *Gazetteer and Directory of Tennessee 1887* does nothing to clarify the matter. This poorly-detailed depiction seemingly fails even to acknowledge the appearance of the recent Centennial Cut-off channel and leaves Corona somewhat "dislocated." Further evidence of the confusion, or at least uncertainty involving the location and political ownership, is found in the "Table of Mid-Stream Distances Between St. Louis and the Sea" contained in the authoritative *The Mississippi River from St. Louis to the Sea* prepared by Ockerson from "reliable sources." This listing shows, at a correct mileage measurement, a landing designated as "Corona, Ark."[9] Tennessee would seem to have lost its settlement regardless of the side of the river considered.

By the beginning of the last decade of that century the earlier "family community" of Corona would seem to have expanded with the diversity of families living in the riverside settlement and with the number and variety of occupations or professions represented. Several business enterprises were evident. An exact total population was not reported, but the community was being provided rather regular mail service, apparently by boat. The *Tennessee State Gazetteer and Business Directory* for 1890 contains the following entry:

> Corona
>   Tipton County
> A landing on the Mississippi river, about 30 miles above Memphis, in the southwest corner of the county
> Mail, tri-weekly. H.M. Stockley, postmaster.
>
> Cooper Mathew, Mason.
> Cotten A, barber.
> Cotton Rev Lee.
> Figgs NG, physician
> Lyons Rev Jonas, blacksmith
> Rattan A S, physician
> Sanders Rev Daniel
> Sanders James, contractor.
> Smith P P, physician.

Stockley C A & Bro, General Store.
Stockley H W, Cotton Gin.
Stockley John T, justice of peace.
Winters James, carpenter.[10]

The individuals credited to Corona in some instances may have included those who owned property outside of the immediate community on other nearby portions of Centennial Island. These persons could have secured mail service through the post office at Corona and identified with the settlement on the basis of a mailing address, as well as a center for supplies and services.

Apparently no articles dealing specifically with Corona or Centennial Island were written or at least preserved during the first four decades of the twentieth century. Perhaps life changed slowly during this period in this area. But maps issued during this period do tell stories. The process of accretion along the northeastern side of Centennial Island during the first decade began to take Corona's riverfront away. By at least 1915, as the new channel shifted generally southward in this area, Corona has lost the use of its previous landing site, and a new Corona Landing had been established about one and one-fourth miles downstream, past the newly-formed sand bar, at the river's edge.

It may reasonably be assumed that the major flood of the early decades of the century posed the same threats to and took the same tolls upon Centennial Island as they did in the case of neighboring Island No. 35 upstream. Another one of the Trigg family descendants, T.G. Uhlhorn, stated in 1940 that he had been familiar with Centennial Island for sixty years. He recalled; "'Only once, in 1927, has the high water prevented us from making a cotton crop. And even then we made a good corn crop.'"[11]

By 1940 Corona Bar had continued it southward expansion to the extent that the community of Corona itself had been left behind about one and one-half miles from the shoreline of the main channel. A short remnant of the earlier channel that formerly served Corona still survived and reached back upstream behind a portion of the bar to within perhaps one half of a mile from the west, but an actual landing was not shown at this location. In the meantime a new formation, the Happy Valley Bar, had developed just downstream and closed access to the shoreline where the Corona Landing had been located. This landing apparently had disappeared or at least lost its map designation by 1940.

Even though Corona itself appeared to have lost its "highway on the river" by this time, the community had found a new avenue to the outside world. Although remnants of the "Old River," the channel that was abandoned after the Centennial Cut-off of 1876, still survived in the form of sloughs farther inland to the north and west, improved roads had been extended from one or more Arkansas communities to the state line and then unimproved roads had been cut across Island No. 37 and Centennial Island to eventually reach Corona and farm homes in the area.

A visitor in 1940 provided a graphic description of a venture into this still rather remote area with the home of the T.G. Uhlhorns, descendants of the Trigg patriarch, as the destination:

> Near Frenchman's Bayou you drive across the levee into the overflow lands, heading straight into what looks like a dense primitive forest.
>
> A sudden turn of the road swings you on to a high, narrow wooden bridge, several hundred feet long, across the Old River...Before it was built, in 1938, communication with [Memphis] was a major problem in transportation.
>
> You roll smoothly over the bridge, the deep, muddy water of an old channel of the Mississippi flowing serenely underneath.... There are thick, dark woods on the other side, but you skirt them and find yourself, without warning, in the midst of the headquarters of as modernized, streamlined a plantation as you could find in the Mid South.
>
> There's the owner's house, a big, comfortable bungalow; there's the manager's house, a pretty cottage; there's the commissary, the barn, the brooder house, blacksmith shop, machine shops, tenant houses, hen houses, sheds and what have you. All the things that are needed for present day mechanized farming, and all are up on stilts or on manmade mounds.
>
> This is headquarters of Happy Valley, largest of the island's three farms....[12]

The soil on Centennial Island by then was already recognized as likely being as rich as any on earth: "Five ears of corn to the stalk, tree top tall, are not unusual, and a bale and a half of lint cotton to the acre is almost the accepted standard."[13]

At that time there were an estimated 500 people on this island of 9,000 acres. Since these inhabitants had the added height and protection for their buildings provided by stilt construction, they rarely had to consider moving to the mainland during high water occurrences. Only during the great 1937 flood, when the river reached an "incredible height, forty-eight feet," did these families abandon their homeland. That year the Happy Valley farm had twenty-six houses swept away, but no lives were lost.[14] Centennial Island was also protected during moderate floods by an elevation that exceeded that of the mainland banks. Usually the Mississippi had to overflow the opposite banks and rise against the distant hills on the Tennessee mainland and the inland levees on the Arkansas side before Corona's island was really endangered.[15]

Walter Stockley Uhlhorn, the son of the owners of the Happy Valley farm, actually was the resident operator. His wife, Aylmarie, had to make some personal adaptations to the isolated life on Centennial when they moved there from Memphis. She recalled the difficulty of travel in earlier years before the connecting bridge had been built:

> 'In bad weather, going to Memphis [forty miles away] meant loading the two babies and all their things into a wagon and driving to Old River. There everything had to be taken out of the wagon and loaded into a boat. Getting the boat across the Old River, if the water was high, was no simple job. Then the children and their things had to be loaded into an automobile. When that was done we had to wait for the trac-

High Ground for Rising River

tors to come and haul the car over the mud to the levee. From there on, there was gravel and highway, and the trip was easy if you weren't too tired to make it."[16]

Law administration during those earlier years was described as having been "on the hit and miss side." To alter that situation, the younger Uhlhorn was appointed justice of the peace for the community. His commissary manager, a man whose last name was Duffle, was added to the force as a deputy. Duffle doubled as the local deputy game warden with the responsibility of protecting geese and duck resources in the area, as well as the fish stock in two fruitful lakes, one of which was the recently formed Corona Lake left by the river's retreat.[17]

Some years later Sam Moore became increasingly aware of the desirability of having telephone service for his home in Corona. Since the telephone company serving the adjoining area of Arkansas was not interested in extending its line to Centennial Island, this determined citizen arranged a connection with the company's nearest point of service out of Joiner, a small Arkansas town northwest of Centennial Island, and laid and buried a cable to bring the line to Corona. He later learned that, since he was still in Tennessee, he was in the telephone market area or jurisdiction of Milligton, a small city located north of Memphis in bordering Shelby County.[18] But any possible extension from the

Substantial, comfortable, beautifully furnished and modernly equipped, the Uhlhorn bungalow is raised above ordinary high water but has to be abandoned when the river goes on a real rampage. [1940]
Reprint from article photocopy as only available source
Permission of The Commercial Appeal

Even the chickens must live high above ground. They learn early in life to negotiate the steep walkway leading to the henhouse. [1940]
Reprint from article photocopy as only available source
Permission of The Commercial Appeal

Decades ago, mules and scrapers piled up this huge mound for the site of Happy Valley's barns. Top of the mound is a little higher than the levee on the mainland so the highest floods have never covered it. When the water rises, the barn becomes on of the island's safety refuges. In 1937 the river was within three feet of the top. [1940]
Reprint from article photocopy as only available source
Permission of The Commercial Appeal

Stilts for everything is the rule on Centennial Island
Reprint from article photocopy as only available source
Permission of The Commercial Appeal

Rulers of "Happy Valley," as the big Centennial Island plantation is called, are Mr. and Mrs. W. S. Uhlhorn, native Memphians. She is the former Miss Aylmarie Pearson. They are shown here at the edge of their lawn where it drops sharply to Mississippi River. [1940]
Reprint from article photocopy as only available source
Permission of The Commercial Appeal

telephone company serving that city and its area would have had the project of running cable under the wide waters of the Mississippi River.

In recent years Sam Moore, who with his brother Horace operate a farm of 2,500 acres on the island, has been confronted with a new obstacle. The U.S. Department of Housing and Urban Development issued a regulation prohibiting property owners within areas designated as floodways from building a residence of any kind. Moore expressed his consternation in this manner:

'When you live on an island, how can you be in any other place than a floodway?

What it amounts to, is that if my house were to burn down, I could not replace it. If my daughter and grandchildren want to build on the island, they could not do so.'[19]

The policy of this department, while wide in attempting to ban "large-scale housing and commercial developments in areas that are subject to flooding" which might otherwise lead to flood disaster relief payments for owners in the event of such calamity, appeared to reflect a lack of first-hand familiarity with "island living." Since Centennial Island is actually higher than the surrounding Arkansas bottom land between the river and the levee, the threat to the Corona area appears to be overestimated by the government officials. Moore even received a letter from a HUD official stating that his house "'impedes the natural flow of the river!'" The Corona resident, whose home is approximately one and one-half miles from the Mississippi, believes that even when the river is up the water that flows through is basement is not "going to hurt the flow of the Mississippi River."[20]

Moore feels that his "high-water house," in reality a "Southern plantation" home according to one writer, is well constructed to withstand any onslaught of Old Man River. The modern brick structure of three stories was built to concede the lowest floor to the flow of the river during flood stage. This lowest level, with an interior constructed of concrete and concrete block, is used only for storage. During one of the worst floods in the history of the Mississippi River, the recent flood of 1975, the swollen river inflicted no real damage. "'We only had ten inches of water in our first floor,'" stated the owner.[21]

This community leader received another letter from HUD. It claimed that inhabitants of islands like Centennial should leave so they could receive an education. Moore believes he has not been too deprived:

'A few years ago, I won the award for outstanding soybean farmer in Tipton County for the highest yield of soybeans per acre. You can't be too uneducated and come up with an average yield of thirty-three to thirty-six bushels per acre.

This year [1977] when cotton crops were poor everywhere, we had a yield of 900 pounds of cotton per acre. In a good year, our yield will run two bales to the acre.'[22]

The Sam Moore estate, along with the nearby homes of his brother and sister and their respective families, serves as the nucleus of modern-day Corona. The sister's house is occupied by the son of the John Tiptons who now reside in Memphis. This modern home is considered to be the structure nearest to the site of the original Corona settlement.[23] It is located on a mound or rise, approached by a series of terraces to give additional protection against occasional high waters when the river returns to overflow Corona Lake which borders the side yard of this home. Once the flood waters crept up the terraces to within four feet of the first floor.[24]

In contrast to the Horace Moore and the John Tipton homes which adjoin the lake that serves as a visible reminder of the river channels's approximate location following the 1876 cut-off event, the Sam Moore home faces westward

Mr. And Mrs. Sam S. Moore Stand On The Balcony Of Their Flood-Safe Home [1977]
Reprint from article photocopy as only available source
Permission of The Commercial Appeal

toward a line of surviving trees fringing the slough that marks the earlier course of the McKenzie chute, once the river's main channel between Island No. 37 and the Tennessee mainland before the cut-off occurrence severed this portion of the Mississippi's lengthy meander.

At present, Centennial Island appears to be an island in name only. The Mississippi River is now approximately one and one-half miles away to the east. A recent estimate of the population, based on 1975 figures, placed the count a approximately 136 or 138 people on the island.[25] The postmaster of the small Frenchmans Bayou, Arkansas post office serving this Tennessee outpost reported about twenty families living "on Corona."[26] In addition to the families of the Moore clan descended from the original Trigg patriarch, about four or five other parties now actually own land on Centennial Island. The old Happy Valley farm is no longer occupied by a Trigg descendent. The other inhabitants of the island are renters who till the fertile farmland.[27]

Today an improved gravel road extends from Corona across the fusion of Centennial Island and old Island No. 37, over the levee into Arkansas, and on to Joiner to the northwest and Frenchmans Bayou to the west, both with easy access to nearby Interstate 55. Tipton County, Tennessee of course still is respon-

139

The Same Moore Home and Estate at Corona on Centennial Island

Courtesy of Thomas H. Anthony

View of Corona Lake on Centennial Island (Earlier channel of the Mississippi River)

sible for local law enforcement from across the river in the county seat of Covington. Likewise the county arranges for the conduct of elections held on Centennial Island.[28] But school children ride out on Arkansas school buses to attend three schools of different grade levels in adjoining Mississippi County, Arkansas.[29]

Corona and Centennial Island live on -- still isolated from their home state and the remainder of their county by the straightened Mississippi River. The residents of this severed lobe are still loyal Tennesseans at heart and some of the leading families maintain close ties with Memphis to the south. However, these inhabitants can neither conveniently nor quickly reach their county seat of Covington across the river to the east. It would seem that these dislocated citizens may in time become increasingly wedded to their neighboring Arkansans as the former realize a continuing and even growing dependence upon the latter for the providing of many of the supplies and services.

141

A FINAL GLIMPSE

Corona, along with Island No. 37 and Centennial Island in general, has experienced no startling changes at last report. The John Tiptons have recently returned from Memphis and occupied their home near the abodes of the other Moore family members. Other than this event little else appears to have changed in the life of this other isolated area of Tennessee.[30]

Endnotes

1. Jan Taylor, "Bureaucracy Invades Island," *Commercial Appeal*, 9 January 1977.
2. St. John Waddell, "Empire On An Island In The Mississippi," *Commercial Appeal*, 21 July 1940.
3. Elizabeth Moore Tipton, telephone conversation with author, 9 September 1980.
4. *Ibid.*
5. Waddell.
6. *State of Arkansas v. State of Tennessee*, 246 U.S. 158 (1918).
7. Joanne Moore, interview with author, Corona, Tennessee, 11 May 1980.
8. Moore, interview; Tipton, telephone conversation.
9. "Table of Mid-Stream Distances Between St. Louis and the Sea" in J.A. Ockerson, *The Mississippi River From St. Louis To The Sea* (St. Louis, 1892).
10. *Tennessee State Gazetteer and Business Directory* (Memphis: R.L. Polk and Company, 1891-92), 209.
11. Waddell.
12. *Ibid.*
13. *Ibid.*
14. *Ibid.*
15. *Ibid.*
16. *Ibid.*
17. *Ibid.*
18. Moore, interview.
19. Taylor.
20. *Ibid.*
21. *Ibid.*
22. *Ibid.*
23. Tipton, telephone conversation.
24. Moore, interview.
25. *Ibid.*
26. Carolyn Speck, letter to author, 6 November 1979.
27. Tipton, telephone conversation.
28. Moore, interview.
29. Speck, letter.

30. Carolyn Speck, telephone conversation with author, 4 October 1984.